MISSING

Missing

The Wartime Account of Two Brothers

DAVID JAMES PARKER

Best Wishes
David Parker.

First published in 2019 by Redshank Books

Redshank Books is an imprint of Libri Publishing.

ISBN 978-0-9954834-5-3

A CIP catalogue record for this book is available from The British Library

Cover and book design by Carnegie Book Production

Printed in the UK by Halstan

Libri Publishing
Brunel House
Volunteer Way
Faringdon
Oxfordshire
SN7 7YR

Tel: +44 (0)845 873 3837

www.libripublishing.co.uk

Disclaimer
Every effort has been taken to acknowledge copyright of images where possible. All other photographs and documents are from the author's collection or with permission of the Warman family.

Dedication

I would like to dedicate this to the memory of Sergeant Harry Warman, Lance Sergeant William Warman and the 600 Gunners Party, May Oakey and George Warman.

David Parker
Kirdford
2018

Contents

Introduction

This book is about two brothers who did nothing heroic except doing their duty. These brothers served in two vastly different places, one in the UK and flying over Europe and the other in Singapore. Harry Warman was in the Royal Air Force and William in the Royal Artillery; both lost their lives during the Second World War. Their story was largely unknown, even to those that knew them, including their brother George. This was partly due to the family being fragmented and working in various parts of the country and world as they moved on – William joining the Army, George going into the building trade, working in Ireland for a period in the 1930s, and Harry joining the Royal Air Force.

Nonetheless, as will become evident in the book, I felt that the story needed to be told. I found a number of people who knew bits about it, but no one knew the whole story. This has led me on a journey of discovery, piecing together these fragments along with the records available. George and his daughter Julie were kept informed of my progress as I went along.

I have had a lot of pleasure in researching this and feel privileged to have been able to tell their story.

I would like this to serve as a memorial to all those mentioned, even though they might not have been direct victims of war. Most of these are no longer with us.

Foreword

My brother was a serving RAF Pilot prior to the Second World War but unfortunately lost his life at the beginning of the war. Due to our family situation and general wartime conditions in early 1940 little was disclosed about the events that led to Harry's demise. I spent many more years wishing I knew about the circumstances surrounding this event and was therefore very surprised to find out from my son-in-law that relatives of Harry's were being traced through the Ed Stewart radio programme. Consequently contact was made with David who informed me about the project to research Harry.

It was very interesting for me to hear about David's knowledge and to have the opportunity to reminisce about the "old days". David's interest and enthusiasm in an historical event affected not only our lives but those of many others and was greatly appreciated.

The researching of events led me to a very welcome reunion with a long-lost cousin and a chance to meet with one of my old school chums after seventy-two years and we spent a wonderful day together at my home. Again this was thanks to David who arranged the get-together and transported my cousins May and Alan.

I am very pleased to know that David has set up a memorial to Harry (The Station Badge of RAF Wattisham as Part of the RAF Heraldry Trust) with the Royal Air Force Heraldry Trust and that his efforts are shared with us in this book.

George Warman

Thank you very much. David
You are very kind it is appreciated George Warman.
& I wish you all the very best.

George Warman

Like Dad I shared an interest in the research into my Uncle Harry. I, of course, never knew him but often heard Dad talking about their childhood, particularly as he and Harry shared their early years being cared for by their grandmother.

I was also present at the reunion with Dad's cousin (whom I had not met until this occasion) and his old school chum and was grateful to David for bringing about this meeting as they all had a wonderful time swapping stories and experiences from long ago. It was the result of David's research into Harry's death that brought about this happy meeting and I was grateful to him for doing so.

I look forward to seeing the finished product and reading the published book.

Julie Weston

William Warman

Harry in RAF uniform

Harry's Mess Tunic

CHAPTER 1

Background

From a very early age I took an interest in history, especially military history. I had heard my father talk about a chap by the name of Harry Warman who had been adopted by Miss May Oakey, his school teacher in Lower Beeding near Horsham.

My interest in Harry came about when, being in need of some pocket money, I used to do small jobs, getting in coal and logs and splitting kindling wood for Miss Oakey on Sunday mornings. This work was always followed by the ritual of sitting down to have a chat with her. Miss Oakey would always have a bottle of Harvey's Bristol Cream sherry and Roka cheese biscuits out and as part of the ritual you always had to join her with a drink – although I was only fourteen at the time. On the bookshelf in her sitting room were two photographs of Harry and his crew (sadly these have gone missing). We started talking about Harry, although unfortunately she did not let much slip! Knowing about my interest in the subject and collecting militaria she gave me Harry's mess tunic and service cap in 1977.

I started then to look for information but did not get very far. In those days it was all done the hard way, with no internet to help. I wrote to the Commonwealth War Graves Commission in 1978 and learnt that Harry was commemorated on the Royal Air Force Memorial at Runnymede, having no known grave. This also gave me his service number and the squadron he served in, with the date of death. Not being able to get access to the personnel records I could get no further, apart from small pieces of information about the squadron.

Fifteen years passed. This is where I started to wonder if the truth was stranger than fiction as I started in earnest. It was while sweeping the chimney for Don and Elizabeth Bateman in Mannings Heath that we spoke about history around that area and Miss Oakey's name was mentioned. Don asked me if the name Harry Warman meant anything to me so I told him what I knew. It just so happened that Elizabeth had worked in the nursing home where Miss Oakey had died. There were no next of kin to claim her personal effects so they were going to be thrown in the bin. As this couple knew her quite well, Elizabeth saved a number of school photographs, diaries, Harry's medals and a Royal Air Force discharge certificate with a pair of pilot's wings.

These had since been passed on, but within a few weeks I had a meeting with Cliff White who gave me the pair of wings, the medals and the discharge certificate. This then gave me the key to unlock the information I needed to continue.

I found out that Harry had been born in Mannings Heath and, with me growing up in Lower Beeding, I knew a lot of people that would have been at school with Harry or would have known about him so I went to see Alan Flint who told me he had lived in his house (3 Jordans Cottages) since 1912 and could remember Harry being born at number 1. Alan also mentioned George, Harry's middle brother, with whom he had spent a lot of time in their youth. I had previously heard about George but Alan went on to talk about William, the eldest son.

Harry's medals: 1939-45 Star, Aircrew Europe Star and War Medal

I then spoke to a number of local people about this and, with my job getting me out and about, I met various other people who knew about Harry.

In the process of finding out about Harry, I wanted also to find out more about John Mahoney his Wireless Operator/ Air Gunner (WOp/Ag) and William Paish. I had an extreme amount of luck with this – or should we say coincidence. On looking for relatives of John I decided to try directory enquiries. There were at the time about fifty Mahoneys listed in Swansea, so I began by asking for six numbers at random. This might seem a strange way of going about it, a needle-in-a-haystack approach you might say, but it just so happened that the first number I tried was John's brother Dan. He had most of the paperwork concerning John, which he very kindly copied and sent to me.

With William's family it was considerably easier. I only had three numbers to choose from and on my second attempt I found William's nephew. Sadly, nothing much came of this contact. In the early days of my research I found another member of 107 Squadron, Sandy Saunders, an aircrew member who knew Harry and his crew. Sandy had been in the RAF since 1930. Having served at RAF Seletar, Singapore for three years he was posted to RAF Miranshah on the North West Frontier where he had his first contact with William Paish and Basil Embry. Sandy flew with Harry a couple of times and on one occasion Harry flew Sandy to Weston Zoyland, Somerset, when he went on leave on 21st October 1939.

My next step was to try to find George!

By early 1994 I had gathered enough information to be able to write a small piece for the local paper. This came out on a Friday morning and as chance would have it I went to my first job that day in Southwater where I had a message to say that a lady up the road wanted to see me. This happened again at my second job in Barns Green – so that took care of my lunch break. I visited Mrs Jones and her daughter May. This was very productive as they had some photographs of Harry in his younger days and told me a few stories about the family. Mrs Florence Jones and May also told me about Harry Jones, May's brother who had joined the Royal Navy and died in 1939. May then told me they had had a letter from George in about 1990. They had done nothing about it and by this time it had gone missing, but May remembered the post mark was Bedford. A clue!

I tried various ways over the next year to find George, not even knowing if he was still alive. This came to nothing. At the time Ed Stewart was doing an afternoon radio show on Radio 2 with a slot called 'where are they now', so in desperation I wrote in to Ed and my request was broadcast. George was found. George's son in law had heard this on the radio. Also that evening George went to his local pub and was told by someone that a chap in Sussex was looking for him. Julie, George's daughter wrote to the BBC and a couple of weeks later I received a letter from the BBC with George's phone number. A lengthy phone call to Bedford followed that evening. Letters then passed between us with more phone calls and a visit was arranged. Tracey and myself took George's cousin with us to Bedford where we met George and Julie – what a great day!

George very kindly gave me letters of permission to gain access to the Royal Air Force records for Harry and the Army records for William. A lot of time was spent talking to George and the story was growing.

The following year I went back to Bedford to to see George but this time Tracey couldn't come with me. I had arranged to take May with me again but still had a spare seat so I invited Alan Flint to come along. This was the first time Alan and George had met for seventy-two years. The stories came flooding out from these two, talking about the fun they had and the people they knew. The first visit to George was special but this one was something really good for me and even better for George and Alan. They had spoken a couple of times on the telephone after I had given the number to Alan soon after I found George. These phone calls carried on for a few years after that.

In 1996 George's half brother Les Richardson, with his wife Doreen, visited from South Africa. He went to see George and two days later came to see me in Billingshurst. He took quite an interest in what I was doing. Although he had met Harry he did not really get to know him that well and did not know the circumstances surrounding Harry's death.

Time has passed and I had the best of intentions to get this published earlier, but as it happens the whole story has grown, finding new information about Harry and enough to include William who was also killed during the Second World War. It may seem rather strange to some people, but I did not know where William was captured in Singapore, but when walking on the beach on Sentosa Island, I had this chill down my spine. Only when I got home did I find out it was at Siloso Fort just behind that beach that he was captured. The internet has helped me latterly with a lot more information released from the National Archives.

It is very unfortunate that George did not know much about William. The family had been split up and after joining the army William was posted overseas for a long period. George was working all over the country as well as in Ireland and so this did not help either. As for Harry, George did see him in 1938 for the last time. It is sad to say that by the time of my second visit to George I actually knew more about his brothers than he did, so I was able to fill in the gaps for him.

CHAPTER TWO

Harry: The Early Years.

Harry was born on 2nd May 1917, the youngest of three sons of George and Bessie (Jones) Warman. He was born at home in 1 Jordans Cottages, Church Road, Mannings Heath. George had served in the Royal Navy during the First World War and then worked as a linesman for the GPO. George died on 10th August 1926. His widow, Bessie, married Joseph Richardson of Mannings Heath in 1927 at Edmonton, London. Bessie had two more sons with Joe. Les and the other one who was known as 'Tiddler'.

Young Harry

Jordans Cottages

William, the eldest son, went to London with his mother while George, the middle son, and Harry lived with their grandmother at North Cottages, Church Road, Mannings Heath. Both George and Harry started at Lower Beeding School. George took the entrance exam for Greenwich Naval School on 14th July 1925.

On the death of Harry's grandmother Harry was adopted by Miss May Oakey of School House Lower Beeding.

Harry was a a popular lad among the other pupils. He was quick to learn and did well, taking the entrance exam for Collyer's Grammar School in 1929. Harry left Lower Beeding School on 28th March of that year.

At Collyer's he was again a popular pupil. Harry was an above-average scholar academically, always finishing the term placed in the top three in the examination lists.

CERTIFIED COPY OF AN ENTRY OF BIRTH

GIVEN AT THE GENERAL REGISTER OFFICE

Application Number 3339891-1

REGISTRATION DISTRICT HORSHAM

1917 BIRTH in the Sub-district of Billingshurst in the County of West Sussex

Columns:-	1	2	3	4	5	6	7	8	9	10
No.	When and where born	Name, if any	Sex	Name and surname of father	Name, surname and maiden surname of mother	Occupation of father	Signature, description and residence of informant	When registered	Signature of registrar	Name entered after registration
246	Second May 1917 Harman's Hill, Kirdford R.D.	Harry	Boy	George Harman	Bessie Harman formerly Jones	Leading Seaman Barracks	A. Harman Father Harman's Hill, Kirdford	Tenth May 1917	L. Savage, Registrar	"Adopted" E. Shaw Mullens Superintendent Registrar

CERTIFIED to be a true copy of an entry in the certified copy of a Register of Births in the District above mentioned.

Given at the GENERAL REGISTER OFFICE, under the Seal of the said Office, the 11th day of July 2011

BXCF 073860

CAUTION: THERE ARE OFFENCES RELATING TO FALSIFYING OR ALTERING A CERTIFICATE AND USING OR POSSESSING A FALSE CERTIFICATE ©CROWN COPYRIGHT

WARNING: A CERTIFICATE IS NOT EVIDENCE OF IDENTITY.

IPS 042424 31535 04/10 3MSPSL 026889

SRM

Harry's Birth Certificate

Harry and Grandmother

Harry took a keen interest in sport, and was captain of various school teams. He was a stickler for fair play. On one occasion Jack Coombes was involved in an incident that was rather brutish: he aimed a most 'ungentlemanly word' in the direction of the opponent and was throughly 'ticked off' by Harry, who was the captain of the junior house team. Harry advised that 'Collyer's School boys do not use that type of language on the playing field'. His sporting interest had been fostered by Miss Oakey who was a keen tennis player and taught Harry and some of the other pupils at Lower Beeding school to play. Harry was also good at putting, winning the Collyer's Old Scholars championship on 29th July 1930 and again in 1931. Harry was also a leading light in the annual school plays. In November 1929 present and old scholars of Lower Beeding School performed a play called 'Revenge – A story of the Afghan Frontier'. Harry played the part of Mahmud-a-Pathan.

Lower Beeding School on the right and
School House on the left

During these early years Miss Oakey used to take Harry abroad. In 1932 they went on a cruise, stopping at Stockholm and Copenhagen (it was from here that Harry sent a postcard to his brother George) with a number of other stops. For Harry this would have been a great opportunity. During these years Harry would make regular visits to see his brother George and cousins at Southwater.

On leaving Collyer's in 1934 Harry got himself a job at Thorneycrofts on an annual salary of £150. This job did not suit him so he left there and registered with the Brighton Employment Exchange. It was while with the Employment Exchange he found his new job as a chemist at the Alpha Cement works in Lewes. In a letter to George he notes how he was lucky to get this job, which had good prospects along with a lot of responsibility, including checking the quality of the cement and other duties. This was very well paid for the time with a starting wage of 30 shillings (£1.50) per week. He had to work shifts, 8am–2pm, 2pm–10pm and 10pm–8am. Harry was travelling fifty-three miles a day to and from work. He had a BSA motorcycle, which was second hand, and made him look like a poor relation compared to his brother and a few of the other chaps he knew who had better machines. (*Ken Sutherland told me this. He recalled that they all used to go about together. Ken also told me that this motorbike is still around and belongs to someone in Storrington.*) Harry obviously had other thoughts about what his career should be and, in 1936, he left Alpha Cement to join the Royal Air Force.

CHAPTER THREE

Early Service

It was on 6th July 1936, aged nineteen years and sixty-six days, that Harry reported to the Superintendent of Reserve at RAF Hendon. Here he was enlisted as Aircraftsman 2, under training Airman Pilot (Group 2) at 1/6d per day. Harry was reclassified as Leading Aircraftsman on 7th July. This reclassification was because he was now a pilot under training. On 31st August 1936 Harry reported to RAF Uxbridge to complete his basic training before being posted to No 2 Flying Training School, RAF Digby. He joined the No 31 flying training course, and flew a mix of Avro Tutors, De Havilland Tiger Moths and Hawker Audax. By May of 1937 Harry had gained his wings and been promoted to Sergeant. This was confirmed on 26th November with his pay rising to 5/- per day. On 26th May Harry was posted to the recently reformed 107(B) Squadron at Old Sarum, Salisbury Plain flying Hawker Hind day bombers. The squadron moved to the Civil School of Aviation at Harwell on 15th June 1937.

During this period the skies of Britain were very busy, with the Royal Air Force training fighter pilots and bomber crews.

The first flying record I can find for Harry is on 25th October, flying Hind K6696 with P/O Temple-West as navigator, when they carried out a low-level raid on Wakes Colne (near Colchester) railway station at 12.30hrs. The flight left Harwell at 11.45hrs and flew in

Hawker Hind

three sub-formations, via Aylesbury, Great Heyford, Dunmow and Broomfield Aerodrome to Wakes Colne. While over the target photographs were taken from 500ft. These, along with the navigator's logs, were taken to the HQ at Upper Heyford (B) Wing. The weather conditions on this flight were very bad.

Similar training was carried out the following day. B Flight were airborne at 06.50hrs (Harry in K6697 with no navigator on this occasion) and flew in a formation of five aircraft led by Plt/Off Harmer; their route went via Alton. They followed A Flight and carried out a raid on Chard railway junction. They returned to Harwell at 08.40hrs. The two flights were airborne again at 10.17hrs (Harry in K6698), with Plt/Off Sisson in K4653 leading B Flight over Upper Heyford, Alton and Bishops Waltham to carry out a raid on Pulborough railway station. With cloud cover estimated at 10-tenths they attacked from 2000ft at 11.14hrs. Harry spent the rest of the day ferrying photographs and navigators' logs to Upper Heyford, clocking 4hrs 10 mins flying time on this day.

Records are sketchy until 25th April 1938 when Harry was admitted to RAF Hospital, Halton after damaging his toes as a result of an aircraft crash while he and some mates carried out some unauthorised flying. During his stay in hospital his brother George went to visit him. George was to see him only once more before Harry was killed. Harry was discharged from hospital after attending a medical board on 13th May. Due to his escapades leading to the accident there was to have been a court-martial but this was dropped due to lack of evidence – it appears that the witness statements varied so much. The pilots involved received a severe reprimand on 16th May. Harry attended another medical board on 15th June to clear him to return to flying duties.

The squadron took part in various training for the next few months, these included calibration exercises for the Observer Corps. These consisted of twelve calibration exercises and twelve service exercises of three hours duration, taking place between 7th July and 26th July 1938. Harry took part in at least one of these on 18th July. Eleven of the exercises were successfully completed and thirteen were affected by the weather. 238 tracks were prepared using the aircraft of Bomber Command. While this was going on some personnel were attached to the Observer Corps monitoring posts to record the observations. The tracks prepared by Bomber Command were then compared with the Observer Corps plots at the operarations centres. Similar exercises were carried out during August 1938 using Blenheims, Battles and Whitleys.

This was all part of the build up of preparations for the possibility of war, with the rise of the Nazi Party in Germany, the constant moves being made by Hitler, the build up and mobilisation of the armed forces and the annexing of parts of Europe.

During 1938 Harry had been classified proficient on Hawker Hart, Hind and Audax, which was somewhat ironic as in September 107 Squadron exchanged its Hawker Hinds for the Bristol Blenheim Mk I.

107 Squadron became part of 2 Group Bomber Command on 28th September and removed its peace-time markings from the aircraft and painted on the wartime code of BZ, (changing to OM on the outbreak of war in September 1939). It is not clear why this change happened. Again irony crops up as this was when Neville Chamberlain and other leaders in Europe agreed to Hitler's demands on the Sudetenland and the famous piece of paper 'Peace in our time' following their Munich meeting.

On 13th November, Harry was involved in his second close shave when his and Plt/Off Rotherham's aircraft collided in mid air. Plt/Off Rotherham was flying Blenheim Mk l L1276, with Harry flying L1292, carrying out formation flying. The cause was Plt/Off Rotherham being temporarily blinded by sun glare. The port airscrew of Rotherham's aircraft struck the wing tip of Harry's, causing damage to the wing tip and aileron. Both aircraft landed safely.

Mk1 Blenheim at Duxford

107 Squadron moved to Wattisham on 11th May 1939 and exchanged its Mk I Blenheims for Mk IVs. With the build up to a war footing the squadron took part in ever increasing amounts of low and high level bombing practices, with long range cross country flights and formation flights, including a number of training flights over France.

Once again Harry was involved with the Observer Corps in 1939, to further links between the RAF and Observer Corps the RAF gave 'Air Experience' flights to Observer corps personnel. Harry took twenty-one members of the Observer Corps up on 15th August, at a time just prior to the RAF taking control of the Observer Corps from the Home Office.

On Sunday 3rd September the Squadron received the news that Britain was finally at war with Germany.

Squadron Hinds K5543, K5558 and K5592

Aircraft in Chapter 3

Serial number K6696 Hawker Hind. Maker's number 7839. Built under contract 424497/35. Issued to 107 Squadron from new on 8th January 1937 and taken on charge by them on the 28th. This aircraft was then taken off strength on 17th March 1938 before being issued to 211 Squadron on 24th March as a reserve aircraft. This aircraft arrived at Aboukir on 28th April and was eventually sold to India with a total of 380 flying hours.

Serial number K6697 Hawker Hind. Maker's number 2241. Also built under contract 424497/35. Issued to 107 Squadron from new on 28th January 1937 and taken on strength on 9th February. This aircraft served its entire – albeit short – life with 107, crashing on 19th August 1938 and being written off on 6th September 1938.

Serial number K4653 Hawker Hind. Built under contract 333273/34. This aircraft was initially taken on strength with Number 1 Aircraft Storage Unit on 20th January 1936. It was issued to 107 Squadron on 21st August 1936 and arrived on 3rd September. On 30th August 1938 the aircraft was taken to 27 Maintenance Unit. The next move saw it going to 25 (Armament) Group where it stayed until 21st May 1940. After a spell in storage while being assessed for suitability for use at a Flying Training School at 52 MU this aircraft was taken to 5 ASU for packing ready for shipping to Kenya. It was taken on strength on 9th March 1941 and was used by a Flying Training School until 31st October 1943 when it was struck off charge.

Serial Number 1292 Bristol Blenheim Mk I. Built by Bristol under contract 527114/36. This was one of the first Blenheims taken on strength by 107 Squadron on 25th August 1938. After being repaired from the mid-air collision in November the aircraft stayed with 107 Squadron until 29th June 1939 when 107 changed to the Blenheim Mk IV. The aircraft went to 5 MU before being passed on to 52 MU on 30th May 1940. At one of these places this aircraft was converted to a Blenheim Mk I Fighter. On 12th June 1940 it was taken on strength by 29 Squadron operating as a night fighter Squadron, and passing to 68 Squadron – also a night fighter squadron – on 3rd February 1941. After a time in storage and repair the aircraft was issued to 42 Operational Training Unit at Andover on 11th December 1941 until December of 1942. The aircraft was moved around between maintenance units before ending up back at 42 OTU on 16th April 1943 where it stayed until it was written off in a crash on 21st September of that year.

Serial Number L1276 Bristol Blenheim Mk I. Built as part of the 527114/36 contract. This aircraft was initially allocated to 21 Squadron and was taken on strength on 18th August 1938. This was short lived with a move to 107 Squadron on 10th November 1938. Shortly after joining the squadron this was the other aircraft involved in the mid-air collision. It was returned after repair and stayed with the squadron until they exchanged Mk I's for Mk IV's in 1939. L1276 then moved to 101 Squadron on 10th October 1939 until suffering another accident on 8th December when it was moved to 50 MU, and then to 4 MU where it was repaired by Cunliffe Owen. From here it served with 57 OTU, 60 OUT Bomber Command and 132 OTU Coastal Command from 31st December 1942 until 12th August 1943. Later used for instructional purposes this aircraft lasted until sometime in 1944 when it was finally struck off charge.

Royal Air Force Ranks

AC 1 and 2	Aircraftsman 1st and 2nd Class
LAC	Leading Aircraftsman
Cpl	Corporal
Sgt	Sergeant
F/Sgt	Flight Sergeant
W/O	Warrant Officer
Plt/Off	Pilot Officer
Fg/Off	Flying Officer
Flt/Lt	Flight Lieutenant
Sqn Ldr	Squadron Leader
Wg Cdr	Wing Commander
Gp Capt	Group Captain
Air Cdre	Air Commodore
AVM	Air Vice Marshal
Air Mshl	Air Marshal
Air Chf Mshl	Air Chief Marshal

Abbreviations

A/A	Anti-Aircraft fire
AFM	Air Force Medal
ASU	Aircraft Storage Unit
BEF	British Expeditionary Force
C/O	Commanding Officer
GPO	General Post Office
Lt Gen	Lieutenant General
MU	Maintenance Unit
Orbat	Order of Battle
OTU	Operational Training Unit
POW	Prisoner of War
Wop/Ag	Wireless operator/Air gunner
W/T	Wireless Telegraphy

CHAPTER FOUR

At War

At the declaration of war the Squadron Orbat read:

"Commanding Officer (C/O) Wing Commander E F Haylock, Adjutant, Pllt/Off Rotherham, Officer Commanding A Flight, W L Stedman and Off Commanding B Flight, G Bearne."

Within an hour of the declaration of war Flying Officer A McPherson of 139 Squadron took off in a Blenheim from Wyton on a reconnaissance mission to photograph German North Sea naval bases. They found concentrations of the German fleet at two of these and the following day found further concentrations. After Fg/Off McPherson's return from his second mission on 4th September ten Blenheims – five each from 107 and 110 Squadrons – left Wattisham to attack German warships at Schillig Roads near Wilhelmshaven. This first raid highlighted the shortcomings of the equipment and organisation within Bomber Command. Of the five aircraft of 107, one returned with its bombs on board and the other four were shot down. This was a heavy price to pay: the loss of four aircraft with ten aircrew dead and two taken prisoner. Aircraftsman 1st Class Larry J Slattery (a great friend of John Mahoney) was the first Bomber Command prisoner of war (sometimes referred to as 'prisoner number one') along with Sgt G F Booth. Fortunately Harry was not included in this raid.

107 Squadron had very little involvement for the next few

weeks. The dynamic Wg Cdr Basil Embry took command of the squadron on 15th September. He brought with him a wealth of experience having been flying in the Middle East previously. The new C/O intensified training and developed tactics so the whole squadron became a more efficient unit.

Although the squadron did take part in a number of reconnaissance sorties and bombing raids I can find no record of Harry taking part in any operations until 29th December 1939 when he took part in a reconnaissance sweep of six aircraft (three from 107 and three from 110 Squadron) over the North Sea to report and destroy enemy shipping. The priority targets within the sweep area were: A: Battleships, B: Cruisers, C: Destroyers and D: Submarines. Photographs were to be taken of any targets attacked. Each aircraft was armed with 2 x 500lb semi-armour-piercing (SAP) bombs.

Led by S/Ldr Saunders they left Wattisham at 10.30hrs, following a route to Pulham, Great Yarmouth and then direct to the sweep areas. Once completed a direct route was the order. Harry was flying P4909 with his regular crew of Sgt Paish as navigator and Sgt Mahoney as WOp/Ag. All aircraft returned at 16.05hrs.

Due to bad weather flying was very restricted during the winter months with most of the airfields in East Anglia being snowbound. The sorties that were conducted were flown in extremely hazardous conditions. Reconnaissance flights only took place on four days between 27th December and 12th January 1940. One of these days was 2nd January when two aircraft of 107 set out from Wattisham at 10.05hrs. The first aircraft (raid BB35) was flown by Fg/Off P E Warne to the islands of Sylt and Amrum to ascertain the existence of balloon barrages on or around the two islands and to look at and photograph the seaplane bases there. Photographs were taken from about six miles out but due to lack of cloud cover Fg/Off Warne did not fly over Sylt. The order was that if there was insufficient cloud cover the sortie was to be abandoned.

Harry was flying the second aircraft(N9190) (raid BB36) with his crew of Sgt Paish and Sgt Mahoney to locate units of the German fleet at Wilhelmshaven. The aim was to ascertain if warships were in the harbour at Wilhelmshaven. No bombs were carried and Harry's orders were to report on battleships and cruisers in Wilhelmshaven as soon as the tactical situation permitted. Any shipping seen on the route out was to be reported on return. Visibility was four to six miles at 9000ft over the North Sea, with 5/10ths cloud cover as they approached Heligoland. At 10.57hrs a vessel was sighted on the port beam steaming in a south-easterly drection. This corresponded with a report by Fg/Off Warne. After climbing to 19000ft three oblique photographs were taken of Heligoland and at 12.03hrs another three 35mm oblique photographs were taken from 23000ft. Four miles east, at 12.10hrs flying over Schillig Aerodrome, no activity was noticed. Harry turned towards Wilhelmshaven at 12.15hrs. Flying south they took five more oblique photographs of the dock area from 23800ft and turned again on a line north-east to south-west, taking line overlap photographs of the harbour. They turned north-north-east with the harbour to starboard and took oblique and vertical photographs. No vessels were seen along the coast until they reached Bauffen Basin where one large vessel thought to be a cruiser or battleship was sighted in the docks. This was later confirmed to be the Tirpitz. One smaller vessel was seen and three smaller vessels were sighted in the outer harbour. Having dropped down to 18000ft approximately fifteen aircraft in two lines were sighted at Spickeroog aerodrome. At 12.40hrs flying at 10000ft, three miles north-north-west of Spickeroog one small and apparently stationary vessel was sighted.

On the return journey at a position of approximately 53 deg.38 min 04 deg.45min three aircraft were seen in formation on an easterly course at approx 12000ft. It is fair to assume that these were Me110s known to be operating in the area although no markings were seen. The three aircraft changed course towards a Blenheim which dived to sea level and the three Me110s were last observed at approx 6000ft on a course of 210deg true and steady. The Blenheim observed was that of Fg/Off Warne who was returning slightly ahead of Harry. At 13.20hrs flying at 200ft one large twin-engined aircraft was sighted at approx 6000ft on a course of 210dcg, again no markings were seen. Fifteen miles off Great Yarmouth ten vessels were seen at 14.00hrs on a course of 120deg. Making landfall at Trimingham at 14.05hrs and reaching Great Yarmouth at 14.15hrs Harry set a course for base returning to Wattisham at 14.35hrs. As a result of this Harry and his crew were mentioned in an official report entitled 'Noteworthy War Services'.

Extract from Bomber Command Routine Orders

Dated 11th January 1940

Noteworthy War Services

Nature of Operation
Reconnaissance of Willhelmshaven and the Vicinity

On the 2nd January, a Blenheim of No 107 Squadron, captained by No 580275 Sergeant H Warman, carried out a visual and photographic reconnaissance of Wilhelmshaven and the vicinity. Successful photographs were taken of Heligoland from 19000ft and of Wilhelmshaven from 23000ft,

*covering the whole of the harbour. The
observer who took the photographs was No
511862 Sergeant W C H Paish and the air
gunner was No 548565 A/C 1 J Mahoney.*

*The task set this crew was successfully carried
out under conditions of extreme cold. The
reconnaisance was carried out with great
deliberation and the whole area well covered
with an 8inch lens. Photographs of great
value were obtained.*

The next operation for 107 Squadron was on 13th January. Harry was flying one of twelve aircraft in a sweep of the North Sea and tasked to bomb enemy battleships, cruisers and destroyers with strict instructions that no other type of shipping was to be attacked but positions, numbers and types were to be noted and reported on return to base. Each aircraft was armed with 2 x 500lb SAP bombs. Leaving Wattisham at 11.40hrs the two flights, one led by W/Cdr B Embry(raid BB41) and the second led by F/Lt Thomson(BB42) crossed the coast at 1204hrs, 4000ft over Great Yarmouth. Flying at 10000ft at 12.42hrs they were over scattered cloud. One aircraft turned back due to engine problems. As the remainder approached the sweep area the cloud thickened. At 10000ft above the cloud visibility was good but nothing could be seen below. Dropping down it was found the cloud base was only 500–700ft. Due to the cloud the sweep was finished and the two flights headed for home. On the return they investigated a British trawler that was off course. Making landfall at Great Yarmouth at 3000ft they made for base landing at 15.00hrs

The next operation to involve Harry was on 27th March when nine aicraft were placed on standby for a reconnaissance and strike force but only seven of these were called on. They left Wattisham at 11.50hrs led by W/Cdr Embry. The object of the operation was to locate and attack units of the German fleet and patrol vessels operating in the vicinity of Heligoland Bight. Two of the aircraft were to fly to the vicinity of Sylt to carry out a photographic and visual reconnaissance of Hornum and List with the object of ascertaining the damage sustained as a result of a night raid carried out by Bomber Command a few days previously. Four enemy destroyers were located off Borkum by W/Cdr Embry and S/Ldr Thomson. A bombing attack was carried out on these ships and their position was reported by W/T. No hits were registered on the ships although some of the bombs dropped within three-quarters of the length of the one of the ships. One cruiser and four destroyers were sighted by Harry. He shadowed them for approximately fifteen minutes and reported their location. A number of attacks were carried out. It is considered that at least one vessel suffered some damage. Most aircraft encountered A/A fire of varying intensity. Plt/Off Murphy carried out a successful photographic reconnaissance of Hornum aerodrome and obtained some valuable photographs. He encountered intensive A/A fire and enemy fighters, but managed to escape into clouds. Flt/Sgt Nichols was not so lucky and his aircraft, Blenheim L8747, was last seen entering clouds with enemy fighters on his tail. Flt/Sgt Nichols was lost along with his crew: Sgt G H Stiles and LAC J B Roberts. On this raid Harry was flying P4864 with Sgt Innes Jones as navigator and Cpl Yeomans as WOp/Ag. Harry returned to Wattisham at 15.40hrs.

7th April saw a force of twelve aircraft take off from Wattisham at 11.30hrs. This was a strike force to intercept an enemy cruiser and six destroyers with the estimation that the interception should be made at 13.24hrs. They were flying in two boxes of six aircraft in fine weather

Blenheim N6192 on ground by kind permission of the
Bristol Blenheim Society

with no clouds and visibility of 30 miles. Within twenty miles of the interception visibility dropped to five miles with 10/10 cloud at 7000ft. On arrival at the estimated point of interception both formations turned onto a heading of 350deg and after four minutes flying on this course the force located seventeen ships of the German Navy including the battleships *Gneisenau* and *Scharnhorst*. In sections of three aircraft they attacked from 6000ft using 12 x 250lb SAP bombs each, no direct hits were observed on either ship but two bursts were seen within 10–15 yards of the *Scharnhorst*. The first two sections attacking from the sun met no resistance but the other two sections encountered intense A/A fire as did the first section when they attacked on their second approach to take photographs. Although no aircraft suffered direct hits, the fire from pom pom shells was sufficiently accurate to force one section to break formation. The pom pom was a multi-barrelled anti-aircraft gun mounted on ships. The shells passed between individual aircraft in the formation. An attack report and message giving the composition, disposition and estimated speed was despatched during the homeward journey. All aircraft returned safely landing at Wattisham at 16.45hrs. Harry was again with his regular crew in N6192 for this mission.

It was later realised that fleet was part of the prelude to the invasion of Norway. Previous reconnaissance flights had shown a build-up of warships and troopships in German ports, and vessels sailing north. Patrols were carried out on a daily basis covering the area of German Bight to Denmark.

Aircraft in Chapter 4

N6190 Bristol Blenheim Mk IV. Built by Bristol under contract 774679/38. This aircraft was taken on charge by 107 Squadron on 20th September 1939. It stayed with 107 Squadron until being badly damaged during a raid on Gravelines on 2nd June 1940. Flying Officer J Stephens crash landed at Wattisham at 07.15hrs. Fg/Off Stephens and his crew of Sergeant W Barrett and Leading Aircraftsman E White survived the crash.

P4864 Bristol Blenheim Mk IV. Built as part of the 774679/38 contract by Bristol it was taken on by 107 Squadron on 9th September 1939. This aircraft's records show that it was at 54 MU at a later date.

P4909 Bristol Blenheim Mk IV. Again built as part of the 774679/38 contract. Although not mentioned in this chapter, Harry did fly this on a couple of occasions. On 14th September 1939 it was delivered to 5 MU. It was then taken on strength by 40 Squadron at Wyton and loaned to 107 Squadron for a while before being returned to 40 Squadron Flown by the squadron commander Wing Commander J G Llewelyn it left Wyton at 10.10hrs on 23rd May 1940 for a raid on Arras/Boulogne. Hit by anti-aircraft fire it crashed between Beuvry and Sailly-Labourse, east-south-east of Bethune. W/Cdr Llewelyn and his Gunner Pilot officer W G Edwards were both killed but the navigator, Sgt J A D Beattie, managed to return to the squadron.

CHAPTER FIVE

Norway

With the German invasion of Norway on 9th April the squadron was flying regular anti-shipping missions. 107 Squadron received orders that, commencing on 15th April, they were to undertake operations against Stavanger aerodrome and seaplane bases along with orders for deployment to Lossiemouth on the 14th. This move also included 110 Squadron who were co-located at Wattisham. The squadron was to be placed under command of the Station Commander of Lossiemouth for day-to-day matters such as discipline and adminis- tration and for operations direct from HQ Bomber Command. The air party of sixteen aircraft and crews were to arrive by 13.00hrs on the 14th with another party of personnel and equipment sufficient to allow one sortie per aircraft before the arrival of the remainder of the squadron. This party was to be moved using civil aircraft. Following a three-and-a-half-hour flight the squadron's aircraft arrived at Lossiemouth in freezing conditions with sleet falling across the area. The ground party of five officers and 100 airmen with the remainder of the equipment left Needham Railway Station at 08.00hrs and were due to arrive at Lossiemouth at around midnight on the 14th/15th.

Although the squadron carried out some operations on the 15th I do not know if Harry took part in any of these. The first one noted is on the 16th when twelve aircraft had been allocated for a raid on Stavanger aerodrome and nearby seaplane base, a distance of 450 miles. In the event it was decided that owing to the possibility of unfavourable weather conditions only six aircraft should go with Harry flying N6192 with Sgts Paish and Mahoney. Two sections took off from Lossiemouth at 06.10hrs led by S/Ldr Thomson. At 6000ft the two sections entered cloud and parted. Ice started to build up on all the aircraft and the formation broke up still further. Continuing to climb, the leader opened out into clear weather at 17000ft and sighted two aircraft below him. S/Ldr Thomson tried to regain the section but two still lagged behind. The aircraft (N6191) flown by Plt/Off Keith D Taute spun down from 15000ft to 600ft due to the weight of ice, and bombs were jettisoned in the sea from 8000ft. Plt/Off Taute mentions in his log book that windows and an escape hatch were blown out and the instrument panel was completely iced up. The leader's aircraft continued to ice up. One aircraft actually hit the water and broke off the tail wheel and damaged the stern frame but as luck would have it the pilot managed to keep control and climbed away. All bar one aircraft abandoned the raid, this being separated from the formation. Those returned flew back independently landing at Lossiemouth between 08.55hrs and 10.20hrs.

The aircraft that continued to the target was OM-H. The pilot, reaching the target flying at 18000ft at 08.55hrs, found the conditions clear with good visibility to the west of the target. The crew observed 50–60 aircraft of various types dispersed around the aerodrome. Eight Me110s were seen to take off from the runway. A low level attack was made from 1500ft using a stick of 4 x 250lb GP bombs. No results were observed due to the fighters taking off. A cruiser was sighted at anchor to the west of the aerodrome. The pilot set course for base making landfall at Aberdeen at 11.00hrs and landing at Lossiemouth at 11.28hrs. It has not been possible to establish which aircraft this was.

Harry and his crew were in action again on the 17th for another raid on Stavanger. Twelve aircraft took off from Wattisham between 09.40hrs and 09.55hrs. On the flight over the North Sea, about 70 miles from the Norwegian coast, seven Heinkel 111 bombers were sighted attacking a British cruiser, *HMS Suffolk*, and four destroyers. These bombers were escorted by Me109s. The Blenheims turned in to give the impression that they were fighters and to try to avoid giving the impression that they were bound for Stavanger. The Heinkels dived into cloud cover following this. The squadron continued to the target approaching at 21000ft and attacked in two flights. Intense A/A fire was encountered and just prior to arrival at the target Me110s. Despite this they managed to inflict a fair amount of damage to the runways and a number of parked aircraft around Stavanger. After bombing a number of encounters with the Me110s took place with the No 3 of the second section being attacked but unaware of the severity of the attacks on the other two aircraft with him. No 3 dived into cloud as did the other two, but from this point No 3 lost sight of the others who did not return to base. No 3 made it back to Lossiemouth with his hydraulic system badly damaged and carried out a wheels-up landing. It was discovered that fifty-three strikes were made on this aircraft. Another two aircraft were attacked by Me110s when about 20–30 miles out to sea but little damage was done. Another was flying along at 3000ft when a He111, mistaking him for a friendly aircraft, formated alongside him. The gunner signalled by lamp and a burst of MG fire was returned from the German bomber. An exchange of shots continued for a while but the German broke off and flew into cloud. The Blenheim received only one bullet.

This encounter led Wg/Cdr Embry to put in a report about the poor defensive armament of the Blenheim, this being a single gun in the wing firing forward and more importantly a single gun in the rear turret. His recommendation was for two in the turret and one in the dished panel, one in each engine nacelle firing rearwards, these two harmonised to cover the blind spot behind the tail, and the forward-firing gun in the wing.

The two aircraft lost on this raid were L9041 piloted by Flt/Lt P Warne with his crew of Sgt N J Griffin and AC1 A J F Golder. The other was N6185 with Fg/Off T V Poltock, Sgt D W Edmunds AFM and AC1 F Harwood; all these aircrew were lost without trace.

On the 19th Harry's aircraft was one of six that took off from Lossiemouth at 10.35 hrs. On approaching the Norwegian coast there was no cloud cover so all six returned to base. Cloud cover was an essential element for protection and enabling the aircraft to approach unseen. An absence of cloud cover would often be the reason to abort a raid. They returned to base, landing at 14.30hrs.

Stavanger was again the target on the 24th when six aircraft including Harry's left Lossiemouth at 01.20hrs, detailed to a diving attack on Stavanger by moonlight. Led by S/Ldr thomson they reached the target at 03.35hrs and attacked with their 2 x 250lb GP bombs and 24 x 40lb GP bombs. The raid was a success with many fires being started. While the second section were running in to attack Plt/Off Murphy's aircraft was attacked by a fighter without result. The blackout on the aerodrome was enforced. Two more Me110s were seen to be operating in the area which led to two further air combats in which Plt/Off Murphy's aircraft was attacked again. This aircraft failed to return with the loss of Plt/Off Murphy and his crew of Sgt D C Durie and LAC E L Weeks. Searchlights were operating round the coast and over the target along with some fairly intense A/A fire. The A/A fire grew in intensity as the raid progressed and consisted of small arms and pom pom types. The remainder returned to Lossiemouth at 05.40hrs.

On the 27th four sections of three aircraft took off between 13.15hrs and 13.40hrs bound for Stavanger again. Ten to fifteen miles out the formation ran into a large bank of fog which was down to sea level – climbing to 10000ft and on top of the cloud and climbing to 12500 ft by 14.55hrs. With the cloud still rising and severe icing starting to cause a problem the formation turned back, landing at 15.55hrs and 16.05hrs.

Although 107 Squadron took part in some more raids on Stavanger on 1st and 2nd May I have not been able to ascertain whether Harry took part in these, though it is quite likely when looking at the number of aircraft involved. On the 1st some of those involved failed to reach the target due to weather and one due to engine failure. The raid on the 2nd was very much the same and only recorded limited success.

It was on 3rd May that 107 left Lossiemouth at 10.20hrs flying a course that took in Montrose, Flamborough Head, Linton, Northampton and returned to Wattisham, landing at 13.40hrs.

CHAPTER SIX

Invasion and Retreat

10th May 1940 saw German forces invade the Netherlands. The Royal Air Force sent out numerous reconnaissance flights to establish the overall picture of the situation. Various raids were mounted by Bomber Command, with 107 taking part in their first raid on the 11th. The German forces moved rapidly forward and by 12th May had reached eastern Belgium. The Netherlands surrendered on the 15th. The invasion force pushed forward into France and the British Expeditionary Force retreated towards the coast.

As the invasion swept deeper into France, the BEF fought fierce battles and rear-guard actions to bring them to Dunkirk. The culmination of these events saw the British garrison at Calais surrounded and the rest of the BEF trapped in a pocket extending about six miles inland from just west of Dunkirk to Nieuport Bains in the east and with their backs to the sea. The situation seemed impossible to escape.

The trapped army not only had the German army to worry about, but the Luftwaffe as well as it sent in numerous attacks with Stuka dive bombers (Junkers 87), normal bombers and fighters. The German Navy at sea also kept up a bombardment to hamper them.

The decision was made to evacuate the BEF. Admiral Ramsay was responsible for Operation Dynamo, the code name given for the rescue of the army from the other side of the Channel. The vast majority of troops were taken from the mole at Dunkirk, but many more were stranded on the beaches. Admiral Ramsay pressed larger vessels into service alongside the Royal Navy to operate from the mole but the larger vessels could not get to the beaches. To this end Ramsey organised a fleet of vessels ranging from river boats and pleasure craft to small sea-going vessels to ferry the men from the beaches to the larger vessels. The armada of bigger ships comprised ferries, paddle steamers, lifeboats and many larger merchant vessels.

On the evening of the 26th the Admiral put his plan into action to evacuate the army from Dunkirk. Within twelve hours the force of ships and small boats had been mobilised. The situation demanded swift action and was responded to by all concerned. The first of these ships to leave was the Mona's Isle on the morning of the 27th, laden with troops. As the day progressed many more ships arrived at the mole and beaches, most of them leaving heavily overloaded with men. The ships leaving faced the combined hazards of the Luftwaffe, the German Navy and mines, some of them sinking soon after leaving with their human cargo. All day and well into the evening, ships were on the move. Many heroic deeds were carried out by the various members involved, including many civilians in their small boats.

This was just the first day.

Royal Air Force Involvement

The Royal Air Force sent an air element to France to try to counter the Luftwaffe and ground forces. A number of Hurricane squadrons took part. These squadrons were temporarily based in makeshift airfields in France and suffered from limited workshop facilities and the lack of spare parts. The bomber element mainly consisted of the obsolete Fairey Battles and Bristol Blenheims. As the situation got worse, so France demanded that more aircraft should be sent over. Air Chief Marshal Sir Hugh Dowding and Winston Churchill resisted these demands, realising that the situation was likely to arise that they would be needed at home; they were not prepared to risk any more valuable aircraft.

The RAF has been highly criticised for not putting more fighters into the battle. The air element in France was by this time being stretched by constant moves back from the front line and running out of serviceable aircraft. It was not until the 27th that Fighter Command put in any show in the defence of the retreating army, sending in Hurricanes and the as yet untried Spitfire operating from bases in southern England. The task of the fighters was to get in and break up the formations of Stukas and bombers. A lot of these actions took place at high altitude and above the clouds of smoke from the beaches or behind the lines so the surrounded BEF saw very little of them, which led in part to the criticism. Still these fighters were in short supply as Air Chief Marshal Sir Hugh Dowding would not commit more than sixteen squadrons at any one time – again, using the argument that they would be needed at home for the defence of Britain. By the end of the day on the 27th the situation was not looking good; the Luftwaffe had done considerable damage but had also lost a number of aircraft. Much is made of the actions of Fighter Command during the Battle of Britain and the fact the pilots were getting very little time to recover, but this was exactly the same situation for those fighter and bomber squadrons based in France and Britain at this time.

Bomber Command had been very much in evidence, sending out both reconnaissance and bombing sorties using Fairey Battles, Vickers Wellingtons, Armstrong Whitworth Whitleys, Handley Page Hampdens and Bristol Blenheims. Based both in France and Britain, losses were heavy: twenty-four Battles and ten Blenheims were lost on the 10th alone. 107 Squadron was operating daily from the 11th to the 17th and again from the 20th; they suffered their first loss on the 12th. The Blenheims of 2 Group Bomber Command put considerable pressure on the advancing German forces attacking troop concentrations, armoured units, motor transport, major road junctions, railways and bridges in an effort to slow down the attack. Bomber Command was stretched to the limit with all available aircraft flying on most days, and sometimes twice a day. Losses were high, the RAF operating over enemy-held territory against heavy A/A fire and the pilots of the Luftwaffe, many of whom had gained battle experience during the Spanish Civil War.

Added to this the Germans stopped short of Dunkirk which, by good fortune, gave a small breathing space to get the troops away. Some of this was because the German Army still relied heavily on horse-drawn transport for supplies and the army had nearly overstretched itself. Additionally, Hermann Goering wanted the Luftwaffe to get some of the credit. The evacuation continued until 4th June by which time 380,000 men had been taken out of France, leaving the rear-guard to make a tactical withdrawal towards Boulogne. Many more had to face the next five years as prisoners of war. One of these was one of Harry's contemporaries from Collyer's, Jack Coombes of the Queen Victoria Rifles.

Telephone lines from France to area command in Aldershot were kept open until July to enable some of the stragglers to be picked up.

Harry with fellow Squadron 107 pilots

CHAPTER SEVEN

In Action over Europe

With the invasion of the Low Countries and France looking imminent, 107 Squadron made their hasty flight back to Wattisham on 3rd May. The squadron had a few days break from operations until the 11th. During this time Wg/Cdr Embry intensified training and had modifications to the Blenheims carried out. This was going to be the start of intensive operations for the whole of 2 Group's bomber force – not to mention the extra work for the ground crews. A host of technicians and maintenance engineers carried out repairs to the damaged aircraft under immense pressure to provide quick turn arounds re-fuelling and re-arming between raids, sometimes twice and occasionally three times a day. Without this extra effort put in by the ground crews nothing could be done. Additionally, all leave was cancelled for RAF personnel and certain civilians in the essential trades. It is clear from the daily routine orders that the station went onto a war footing with more guards being posted at various points and duty pilots being detailed.

Harry's first operation was on the 14th flying N6191 with his normal crew. Eighteen aircraft, a mix of 107 Squadron and 110 Squadron took off at 16.15hrs with Wg/Cdr Embry leading to attack advancing German troop transports and armoured vehicles on the road to Givonne and Bouillon as well as in the wood a quarter of a mile to the west of Givonne. Alternative targets for this raid were the river crossings at Sedan with the objective to create a road block or disrupt movement and to attack villages east and west of Sedan between Vrigne and Dovey. The squadron flew to the Kent coast where they were to meet up with an escort of Hurricanes for the attack. This was the first time that the bombers had a fighter escort. Policy between the wars had been that it was not an economical use of fighters to escort bombers.

This was only a small part of a much larger operation with other Blenheim squadrons operating out of bases at home and France along with a number of Fairey Battle squadrons operating out of French airfields in the Sedan area. Losses were extremely heavy.

Flying out the weather was hazy with visibility of about ten miles closing down to six miles near the target area. One of 107's aircraft returned to Wattisham with engine trouble, the remainder carried on to the target. The three main targets were attacked successfully with the alternative targets also being attacked. Bombs were seen to burst in Sedan, north of the river and on houses on the Bouillon-Givonne road. Very intense and accurate anti-aircraft fire was encountered with tracers and explosive shells. Around the target area twenty Messerschmitt Bf109s were operating, making successive attacks on the bombers. 110 Squadron lost five of their aircraft around the target area due to A/A fire and fighters. The air gunners of 107's Blenheims put up a good show with one bringing down a Bf109 which was seen to emit smoke and dive into the ground. Another 109 was hit and badly damaged but the final result was not seen. A Storch observation aircraft was sighted near the target area as was a silver-coloured balloon in a wood three miles north-east of Sedan.

All of 107's aircraft returned to Wattisham, Harry landing at 20.05hrs. Every aircraft suffered extensive damage which meant that the squadron was non-operational until the 18th.

From the 20th the squadron was flying two missions daily. Following a reconnaissance flight at 05.00hrs on the 20th, 2 Group sent an order for the aircraft of 107 and 110 Squadrons, along with aircraft of 21 squadron based at Watton, to attack an enemy column whose advanced elements were in Arras with the main body of the force at Marquion. Harry, flying his usual N6192 with the normal crew, left Wattisham along with the others of 107 and 110 at 09.00hrs, making their rendezvous with the Blenheims of 21 Squadron over Wattisham. On this occasion three Hurricanes were flying with the bombers as escorts. The Blenheims flew from Wattisham to Manston to rendezvous with the Hurricanes at 10.40hrs. The aircraft arrived over the target at 11.25hrs and bombed from 6500ft the enemy motorised column which extended about 300 yards either side of the village of Vis-en-Artois on the Cambrai-Arras road. Bursts were seen on the column and the road junction in Vis-en-Artois. Anti-aircraft fire was encountered but this was light and not close enough to create a problem. All the aircraft returned safely, with 107 and 110 Squadrons landing back at Wattisham at 12.30hrs.

The same aircrews were called on once again on the 20th, taking off at 17.30hrs. This was to attack an unspecified column of enemy that had advanced at Frevent towards Abbeville or on the road from Frevent to Montreuil with special care being taken not to bomb refugees. The secondary target was again an unspecified column moving northwards on the Bapaume-Arras road, with an alternative of any favourable target in the triangle of Arras-Cambrai-Albert but avoiding bombing the towns themselves. A rendezvous with Hurricanes of 3 Squadron at Hawkinge provided escort to and over the target after which they were to go on an offensive patrol. Arriving over the target between 18.30 and 18.35hrs vehicles were seen in Ervillers which was bombed from 6000ft. While over the target area A/A fire was heavier this time but still no damage was done. The Hurricane escort attacked a Henschel 126 which was seen to crash. All the aircraft landed at Wattisham at 20.10hrs.

On the 21st an order received from 2 Group at 07.50hrs was for all available aircraft to be on standby from 09.00. This changed and four sections took off from Wattisham at 08.20hrs. A major crisis was reported at Abbeville. The Germans were approaching along the Frevent-Abbeville road (20 miles west of Arras). The order was to attack everything seen along this road. Approaching the target at 09.35hrs at a height of 6000ft the squadron encountered moderate flak which was accurate. Six aircraft were hit but only lightly damaged. The roads were heavily congested with enemy infantry and motor transport along with horse-drawn transport, mixed with refugees. It was difficult to identify friend from foe. Once located the squadron bombed the enemy troops. Parts of Abbeville were seen to be burning from the German attacks. Auxi-le-Chateau was also bombed on this raid with bursts seen on the edges of the town, which was congested with enemy troops. After taking a number of reconnaissance photographs the squadron headed back to Wattisham, landing at 10.30hrs.

On landing, the aircraft were immediately refuelled and re-armed in readiness for further action. This was Harry's first operation of the day. It is not clear which of the following raids he took part in so I have included both.

At 16.45hrs eleven aircraft, a mix of 107 and 110 Squadrons, left Wattisham to attack infantry, tanks and motor transport 15 miles south of Boulogne proceeding north. 107 Squadron was to meet up with a fighter escort of Hurricanes over Boulogne. If the enemy could not be located here they were to search along the

Etaples-Montreuil-Hesdin roads. Many refugees were fleeing the advancing Germans so care had to be taken not to bomb them by mistake. A column of motor transport was found south of Hesdin on a crossroads at St Austreberthe. From a height of 6000ft bombs were dropped onto the road and into the woods where transport was in cover. Moderate anti-aircraft was encountered which had little effect. The aircraft landed back at Wattisham at 18.55hrs with no casualties.

At 18.45hrs another six aircraft took off from Wattisham to attack a parked up convoy on the Montreuil-Samer road bombing from 1000–1500ft. Five aircraft attacked this convoy with the bombs seen to overshoot the target with no result. Two of the aircraft then attacked a convoy three miles north-west of Samer with much better results this time – at least four fires were seen within the convoy. A further aircraft then attacked another smaller convoy

Bristol Blenheim Mk IV

with one of the bombs missing the convoy but hitting a tank parked in a field. On the return a bridge over the river at Etaples was seen to be packed with civilian traffic heading south. The bridge had a large hole in one end but not enough to stop the flow of traffic. Numerous enemy lorries were seen in the Samer-Desvres-Hucqueliers-Montreuil area with two small fires in a village and a large fire was sighted at Longfosse. Again there were no casualties on this occasion, with all the aircraft landing at Manston at 21.15hrs.

Late morning of the 22nd Flt Lt Pleasance left Wattisham for a reconnaissance sortie over the areas of St Valery-Amiens-Poix-Aumale-Blagny-Eu-Neufchapel and Dieppe. Arriving over the St Valery at 13.50hrs he sighted a column of enemy transport. On the road from Eu to Dieppe he saw a large number of refugees, and at Amiens he saw that the town was badly damaged and burning. Flying out to sea he spotted a ship that was burning and sinking, three miles west of Boulogne, this was thought to be a British vessel.

At 16.10hrs five aircraft left Wattisham with Harry in N6192, for the area that had been recce'd in the morning. Arriving over Samer about forty transports and a number of tanks were seen about two miles south of the village. The area was defended by approximately thirty anti-aircraft guns, whose fire was intense and accurate. Before reaching the target, Plt/Off Millar's aircraft was hit by A/A fire. One engine and the hydraulic system was put out of action and the other engine damaged. Millar did not attempt to land in France lest he and his crew should become POWs. He took the decision to attempt to reach the English coast. However, his second engine failed, some miles from the English coast and he put his aircraft down into the Channel about seven miles from Dover. The crew took to the dinghy. Millar and his navigator, Sandy Saunders, were both injured by shrapnel and his gunner was badly shaken by the experience. All three recovered from their wounds but Sandy was not to fly again as a result of this experience.

Wg/ Cmdr Embry's aircraft was thrown upside down by A/A fire. He sustained a large hole in one of the wings. With great difficulty he managed to fly back and land at Hawkinge. On the way nearing Dover he became the target of friendly fire from the Royal Navy, luckily their aim wasn't good and no damage was done.

The remaining five aircraft, after completing a reconnaissance, climbed to 6000ft and then carried out an attack on the enemy columns. Some excellent results were observed with direct hits being scored on the motor transport, many of which were thrown off the road and into nearby fields. It was considered that a great deal of damage was done on this raid. The aircraft submitted their report by W/T to Wattisham on their return journey, landing back at their bases at 18.25hrs.

Overlapping this attack another flight took off from Wattisham to hit the same area. Aircraft from 107 and 110 Squadrons, set off again on the 22nd to attack more transport in the vicinity of Samer and Tingry. Although Harry was not part of this it does serve to illustrate the demands being placed on Bomber Command and especially the medium bombers of 2 Group. The order was to bomb fifty vehicles on the road between the two towns. They found this column on the road and some parked up in Samer. Some of the flight bombed these and when done moved on to Tingry where they found forty vehicles moving along the Samer-Montreuil road two miles south of Tingry. Another group of stationary vehicles was also attacked, one mile west of Samer. On the return journey they flew over a village between Samer and Tingry that had been attacked earlier where they saw several fires. The results were good. Anti-aircraft fire was moderate but not terribly accurate. The aircraft landed back at Wattisham at 21.00hrs.

Taking off from Wattisham at 20.05hrs, Harry's second mission was as part of a formation of six aircraft to attack the headquarters of the German 9th Armoured Division at Ribeaucourt. Encountering moderate but accurate A/A fire on the way, they arrived over the target at 21.00hrs and made a level bombing run at 8000ft. Most of the bombs fell within the village starting a number of fires. This was regarded as a most successful attack. Visibility over the target was down to two miles with the light failing. The flight made its way back towards home and due to the darkness landed at Manston. Leaving Manston in the early hours of the 23rd they arrived back at Wattisham at 08.25hrs.

On the Daily Routine Orders for 23rd May was a special message from the King.

> *'The following message has been received from His Majesty the King'.*
>
> *During my visit to the Headquarters of Bomber Command today, I was able to hear more about the epic deeds of our Bomber forces in the recent weeks, coupled with the arduous and unceasing duties of the Coastal Command and with the heroic exploits of our Fighter Squadrons in this country and in France, they make an immortal story, a story that fills the whole Empire, whose sons are now fighting in all three branches, with gratitude and admiration.*
>
> *I congratulate the Royal Air Force with all my heart and wish them good luck and continued success. The matchless spirit that has shown*

so clear an ascendancy over the enemy makes the final victory for the Allies doubly sure.

Signed George RI   18/5/40

A message from HQ 2 Group on the morning of the 24th gave little time to get ready. Along with six aircraft from 110 Squadron and two other Blenheim squadrons six of 107's aircraft took off at 14.10hrs. They were to attack armoured cars, tanks and motor transport between St Inglevert and Coquelles, to be over the target at 13.00hrs. Just before crossing the French coast, warships thought to be cruisers were seen burning. Fires were also seen in Boulogne and around the docks. Coquelles was seen to be burning from German attacks on the village – the German Army were doing a lot of damage. Two miles north of Boulogne fifty vehicles were sighted, parked up and spaced at about fifty yards apart, facing north. A number of A/A batteries were seen in the north of the forest of Boulogne south of the Boulogne-Colembert road. The fire from these was quite intense.

On the roads from St Martin to Marquise and Hauteville scattered enemy transport was sighted but the primary target could not be found, as the enemy had moved by the time the bombers arrived. So the leader took the decision to return to the A/A batteries and bomb them. The guns were silenced with the full bomb load of the twelve Blenheims. The aircraft arrived back at Wattisham at 16.00hrs. On landing the aircraft were refuelled and re-armed ready for the next attack.

Harry was airborne again at 20.00hrs when the same twelve aircraft, with more aircraft from Watton, took off to attack 200 enemy tanks reported on the road between Oye and the bridge to the west of Gravelines. Before reaching the target enemy A/A fire was encountered at

Port de Oye and again at Marck. One of the Hurricane fighter escorts was shot down by anti-aircraft fire five miles south of Marck. Arriving over the target at 6800ft at 20.34hrs the majority of the aircraft bombed the tanks. Extensive damage was done with fires being seen on the western edge and the road to the north-east of the town. The remaining aircraft with bombs returned to Marck where some of them bombed the A/A batteries and silenced them and the others bombed the canal bridge at Marck from 7000ft. With the onset of evening it became too dark to carry out reconnaissance and so no photographs were taken of the targets. Some of the aircraft were damaged by the anti-aircraft fire encountered but all managed to return to base, landing at 21.30hrs.

In the daily routine orders for the 24th was a special message:

"The French Minister of Information conveyed to Mr Duff Cooper on the 18th May 1940, his personal appreciation and the appreciation of every Frenchman of the heroism of the Royal Air Force which would be a decisive factor in saving France". (This may have been slightly premature considering the events that followed with France being occupied for nearly four and a half years. Author.)

Although extremely likely, when we consider the number of aircraft involved, I have not found any firm evidence that Harry was flying on the 25th and 26th but I have included an outline of the attacks made by the squadron.

On the 25th a message was received from HQ 2 Group to bomb bridges across the River Lys between Menin and Courtraiat at the request of General Georges who was 'in a hell of a hole'. Twelve aircraft from Watton and twelve from Wattisham were tasked with this. Meeting up with a fighter escort at Hawkinge they set course for the target bridges over the River Lys at Herelbout, Pas de Calais, half a mile north-west of Marck. The bridges were successfully attacked with all being breached and the formations landed back at 18.00hrs.

On the 26th twelve aircraft of 107 and six of 110 Squadron took off at 17.40hrs to attack enemy vehicles in the Forest D'Hesdin, on the road and at road junctions, with the additional target of vehicles at St Pol. Again a successful attack was carried out with reconnaissance being carried out on the return journey. All aircraft landed back at 19.55hrs.

Between 4th September 1939 and 3rd May 1940 107 Squadron had lost nine aircraft, with twenty-eight aircrew killed and two made prisoners of war. Between 11th and 26th May they lost a further five aircraft with seven aircrew killed, four made prisoners of war, and five injured. Of those injured, one was so badly wounded he could not return to flying while the other four returned to flying once they had recovered from their injuries. One of those who returned to flying was Flg/Off R C Rotherham who had been involved in the mid-air collision with Harry before the war. Flying L8748 OM-K he was shot down by Bf 109s on an operation to Maastricht on 12th May. Rotherham made a forced landing in a part of Belgium that was still in allied control. Along with Rotherham, Sgt R Brown returned to flying while LAC C E Coote, who had received leg injuries, was taken prisoner while still in hospital.

Aircraft in Chapter 7

N9191. Bristol Blenheim Mk IV. Built by Bristol under contract 774679/38. Taken on charge by 107 Squadron on 21st June 1939, the aircraft remained with them until 1st October 1940, when it crashed on take-off and burst into flames at Wattisham. Sgt Walters (air gunner) was pulled from the wreckage and eventually recovered from his injuries. Sgt J E Merrett and his navigator were not so fortunate and died in the fire. Wg/Cdr Sinclair was at the scene and displayed outstanding courage. He was awarded the George Cross for his actions.

Chapter Eight

The Crash

Squadron Leader Stokes was posted to 107 Squadron on 27th May and was promoted to Wing Commander on taking command of the squadron. Wg/Cdr Embry now promoted to Group Captain – handed over to Stokes in the morning and was due to go on leave before he started his next posting as Station Commander at West Raynham.

At 17.45hrs a message was received from 2 Group stating that a column of enemy motor transport and armoured vehicles were passing through St Omer on the road to La Payellette[1] and thence along the road south of the Foret de Rihault-Clairmarais or to Maloive and skirting the forest. The purpose of the raid was to destroy the enemy vehicles and armour. The order went on to give details of attacking when the enemy left St Omer by the southern exit or when passing through Arques or La Payellette. It was essential not to attack these areas unless movement was seen.

No 2 Group wanted six sections despatched to attack these targets. It was deemed essential to press home the attack. As stated in the previous chapter the BEF were under considerable pressure and the evacuation had started so it was of high importance to slow down the German advance. No fighter escort was to be provided on this raid, as had been the case on some previous raids. Pilots were instructed to use cloud cover where possible. No 2 Group wanted visual reports sent back by W/T as soon as it was practical.

On receipt of this order Embry discussed with Stokes the possibility of leading the squadron for one last time, with Stokes taking command on their return.

Between 18.00hrs and 18.15hrs twelve aircraft of 107 Squadron took off from Wattisham, followed at 18.25hrs by six aircraft of 110 Squadron, who were also back at Wattisham after their short time at Lossiemouth. The twelve aircraft of 107 Squadron were captained by:

Wg/Cdr Embry (flying L9391)

OM-F, Fg/Off Stephens,

Plt/Off Carter,

Sqn/Ldr Stokes,

Sgt Warman (in N6192 OM-E with Sgt Paish and Sgt Mahoney),

Plt/Off Taute,

Flt/Lt Pleasance,

Fg/Off Bomford,

Fg/Off Roe,

Plt/Off Murray,

Plt/Off Bennett,

Plt/Off Mitchinson.

The six sections crossed the coast at Ramsgate and headed out across the English Channel towards St Omer. While crossing the Channel a ship was sighted almost on its side and burning fiercely. This was quite likely to have been the small coaster *Sequacity* which had been a target of enemy bombers. Approaching the French coast the crews could see great palls of smoke from the docks and beaches of Dunkirk. The weather from mid-Channel was 3/10ths cirrus cloud with visibility of about 20 miles. The squadron crossed the coast at Gravelines at about 1840, flying at 7000ft. Many Bf109s were seen in the area. Anti-aircraft fire was so heavy and accurate that it was possible to follow the formation by the black smoke from the A/A bursts.

Arriving over St Omer between 18.45hrs and 19.10hrs all but two aircraft bombed the targets west of St Omer and in the forest at Clairmarais, from 4500–5000ft. One aircraft was forced to take evasive action from one of the numerous enemy fighters in the vicinity and so failed to bomb the target, while another had problems with the bombs "hanging up" (this is a failure for the bombs to release). Bursts were seen on the road at various points within the distance of about a mile. Soon after Embry dropped his bombs his aircraft received a direct hit from the A/A fire and he lost control. Embry and Sgt Whiting his navigator managed to bail out, but they were the only two to escape from the doomed aircraft. Sgt Lang, his WOp/AG was seen to be dead in his turret. Embry's aircraft was seen by the rest of the squadron to rapidly gain height near Nordausques at about 18.50hrs and two parachutes were seen at about 7500ft. Later in the day Embry and Whiting were captured. Embry was taken to General Guderian who admitted that the bombing was causing heavy casualties. Despite this the General lent Embry his overcoat to keep warm.

After bombing, a visual recce was carried out to assess the amount of German activity in the area of the Watten-Gollezelle, Watten-Cassel and Rummingham-Watten roads from 5000ft. The movement of vehicles was virtually continuous, heading in an easterly direction. The squadron was back in action on the 28th to attack these targets.

Still experiencing intense A/A fire, the formations headed back to the coast, led now by Stokes, with three Bf109s on their tails. One of the Bf109s attacked a Blenheim from astern but broke off the engagement after several bursts of return fire from the rear gunner. On nearing

Dunkirk one of the Bf109s was seen to attack Harry's Blenheim from close range. White smoke was seen to come from one engine. Harry crashed into the sea about seven miles out from the coast at Marck in the Pas de Calais. It is not entirely clear what the exact circumstances were, but the reports state that only one Bf109 attacked Harry but add that three German pilots claimed shooting down a Blenheim around this time. The three pilots were Rudolf Goy, Eduard Berwanger and Artur Trutwin of 5/JG53.

In the last paragraph of his book, *Wingless Victory*, about Embry's (later Sir Basil Embry's) escape from France, Anthony Richardson, the Adjutant of 107 Squadron writes:

"Five thousand feet above and several miles away, Wg/Cdr L R Stokes, with two of his crews lost, gathered his brothers around him in the mid-sky, fought off the swarming German fighters and led the remaining element of his squadron safely home."

The ten aircraft of 107 Squadron landed back at Wattisham at 19.30hrs, followed by the six aircraft of 110 Squadron at 19.55hrs. Although on some previous raids all the aircraft had suffered some sort of damage, these had been the worst conditions the squadron had encountered as far as A/A fire and enemy fighters were concerned up to this point in the war.

[1] *French place names are as they appear in the Operational Record Book of the time, EXCEPT where there has been an obvious typographical error.*

Aircraft in Chapter 8

L9391. Bristol Blenheim Mk IV. Built under contract 551920/36 by Rootes Group. This aircraft was issued to 27 MU on 13th February 1940 and taken on charge by 107 Squadron on 10th May 1940. It was shot down over the target near Nordausques on 27th May 1940.

N6192. Bristol Blenheim Mk IV. Built under contract 774679/38 by Bristol. Initially in storage at Waddington from 9th May 1939 until it was taken on charge by 107 Squadron on 21st June 1939. It crashed into the sea seven miles from the French coast on 27th May 1940.

CHAPTER NINE

Missing

The school day had already started on 28th May 1940 when Miss Oakey received the telegram from the Air Ministry to inform her that Harry had been posted missing. (Miss Oakey along with his brother George was his next of kin.) This of course came as a total shock to her – total devastation according to some of the pupils at the school. Miss Oakey immediately closed the school for two days while she tried to come to terms with the news. Under normal circumstances this would have been totally unheard of but many of the pupils knew Harry or had seen him around while he was on leave. He was well respected by all and the RAF had an air of glamour about it. Being a handsome chap he was also well liked by the girls. (I found this to be a common theme with the majority of people I have met during my research.)

It was not until 30th May that George received a letter from the Royal Air Force Records Office informing him that Harry had been posted missing. Sadly now George has only half of the letter. It reads as follows:

> 'Dear Sir. I presume that by now the news of your brother No 580275 Sergeant Harry Warman of No 107 Squadron, Royal Air Force, is missing has already reached you.
>
> May I assure you of the sympathy felt ...'

The information was telegraphed to his guardian, Miss E M Oakey, The School House, Lower Beeding, Horsham, Sussex, whom he had nominated as the person to be informed should he become a casualty. This is all George

Letter to Ms. Oakey

Dept. Q.J.

P.352477./40/P.4.Cas.

27 February, 1941.

Madam,

    I am commanded by the Air Council to state that in view of the lapse of time and the absence of any further news regarding 580275 Sergeant H. Warman since the date on which he was reported missing, they must regretfully conclude that he has lost his life, and his death will be presumed, for official purposes, to have occurred on the 27th May, 1940.

    The Council desire me to express again their sincere sympathy with you in your bereavement and in the anxiety which you have suffered.

    I am, Madam,

    Your obedient Servant,

Charles Evans

Miss E.M. Oakey,
  School House,
    Lower Beeding,
      Near Horsham,
        Sussex.

had left of the message. As George stated in the Foreword of this book, very little was disclosed at the time. He had always thought that Harry went missing while on ops over Norway. It was not until I got in touch with George in January 1995, following detailed research that he found out the whole story.

Flight Magazine on 4th July reported that Harry was posted missing along with William Paish and John Mahoney. The others mentioned, who were shot down on the same day were W/Cdr Basil Embry, Stg Lang and Sgt Whiting.

On 26th July the *West Sussex County Times* ran the Old Collyerians Honours List, which gave details of those "old boys" serving in the Forces. It read that eighteen had been safely taken off the beaches at Dunkirk and four were posted missing, one of these being Harry along with Jack Coombes of the Queen Victoria's Rifles (who was mentioned in the introduction) who had been captured as one of the rear guard and spent the rest of the war as a POW.

The Collyerian (the school magazine) summer edition, Vol VI No 54 had an entry for Harry noting that he was posted missing on 28th May after raids on the Calais–Boulogne area. He had been in service almost continuously from the start of the war. It goes on to say that he was mentioned in official reports for reconnaissance in severe weather in January and was soon to receive his commission.

There was no news from the relevant agencies of Harry becoming a Prisoner of War or evidence of him returning to this country. This, and the absence of a body, meant that the Air Council had to presume that Harry had lost life when his Blenheim went down.

CERTIFIED COPY OF AN ENTRY OF DEATH   **SA** 081108

Application Number 3914348/1

Registration of Births, Deaths and   Marriages (Special Provisions) Act 1957

Return of Air Force Personnel Killed in Action or who have died while on Service Abroad
In the War of 3rd September 1939 – 30th June 1948

Name in Full (Surname First)	Rank and Unit	Age	Country of Birth	Date of Death	Place of Death	Cause of Death
WARMAN Harry	Sgt. 580275 107 Sqdn.	23	England	27.5.1940 Presumed	Lost at sea	Air Operations

An entry relating to the Death of............. Harry Warman

CERTIFIED to be a true copy of *the certified copy of* an entry made in a Service Departments Register.
Given at the GENERAL REGISTER OFFICE, under the Seal of the said Office, the   day of   **14th**   **March 2012**

If the certificate is given from the original Register the words "the certified copy of" are struck out.

Section 3(2) of the above mentioned Act provides that "The enactments relating to the registration of births and deaths and marriages in England and Wales, Scotland and Northern Ireland (which contain provisions authorising the admission in evidence of, and of extracts from, certified copies of registers and duplicate registers) shall have effect as if the Service Departments Registers were certified copies or duplicate registers transmitted to the Registrar General in accordance with those enactments."

CAUTION: THERE ARE OFFENCES RELATING TO FALSIFYING OR ALTERING A CERTIFICATE AND USING OR POSSESSING A FALSE CERTIFICATE
©CROWN COPYRIGHT
WARNING: A CERTIFICATE IS NOT EVIDENCE OF IDENTITY.

Harry's Death Certificate

Dated 27th February 1941, the letter to Miss Oakey states that due to the lapse of time and the absence of further news regarding 580275 Sgt Harry Warman since the 27th May 1940, on which he was posted missing, the Air Council … "must conclude that he lost his life and that his death will be presumed, for official purposes, to have occurred on the 27th of May 1940." This follows through on his Certificate of Discharge:

> Certified Discharged 27th Day of May 1940
> Killed in Action.

Probate was passed at Lewes, Sussex on 7th December 1940. His estate being valued at £128 and probate was granted to Miss Elizabeth May Oakey, spinster.

Although the following came in after 27th May I feel it relevant to include this:

> Message addressed to the Air Officer Commanding-In Chief, Bomber Command, from Air Ministry, on 4th of June 1940.
>
> Please convey to all ranks in your command the following message from the Secretary of State: The War Cabinet have expressed their high appreciation of the fine work of the Royal Air Force in covering the evacuation of the British and French Forces from Dunkirk. All ranks have done magnificently. In this trial of strength with the enemy the pilots and crews of our aircraft have gained an ascendancy over the German Air Force. They have inflicted on the enemy losses far heavier than our own, and they have played an indispensable part in preventing the destruction of the British and French Armies in Flanders. Through the battle our aircraft have operated with unparalleled intensity, sustained by the sure skill and un-wearying work of the ground personnel. All ranks have worthily upheld the traditions of the Royal Air Force and have earned their country's gratitude.
>
> Archibald Sinclair.
>
> (Secretary of State for Air).

CHAPTER TEN

The Crew

Although on more than one occasion Harry flew with other crew members, his normal crew and the crew that he died with are the ones I will mention in this chapter.

511862 Sergeant William Charles Henry Paish

William Paish was born in 1912, the son of William T and Sarah A Paish. He lived at Aldsworth, Gloucestershire. William joined the Royal Air Force in 1931. He was serving with No 9(B) Squadron at Boscombe Down in July 1932. Later he served in the Middle East and then on the North West Frontier, Afghanistan. It was on one of these postings that he first met Basil Embry, and Sandy Saunders also knew of him at this time. Sandy was a professional airman, navigator, having joined the Royal Air Force in the early 30s. William's second flying log book starts on 6th August 1935 and shows that he had flown some 1,028 hours. On the return journey he happened to bump into his brother who was travelling out there, again with the RAF. William was Harry's navigator, his first flight with Harry was on 2nd May 1939 and he became a regular member of Harry's crew from 1st September 1939. It is noted in Daily Routine Orders dated 11th May 1940, RAF Wattisham, that Sergeant Paish was to be Duty Pilot on the 12th. I have found no other record of him being a pilot. William is commemorated on Panel 18 of the Royal Air Force Memorial at Runnymede.

548565 Aircraftsman 2nd class. John Mahoney

In the text I have referred to John as Sergeant. The reason for this is that it was around May of 1940 that all aircrew were given the rank of Sergeant, but his record still has his rank as AC 2.

John was born in the parish of St Josephs, Swansea on 26th October 1920, son of Cornelius and Johanna Mahoney. John joined The RAF on 3rd February 1938 at the age of seventeen years and 101 days. His trade was Aircraft-hand u/t Wireless Operator (Group 5). His description is:

Height: 5ft 7in.

Chest: 31in.

Hair: Brown.

Eyes: Blue.

Complexion: Fresh.

With two vaccination scars on his left arm.

John was enlisted at RAF Cardington, Bedfordshire. On completion of his training John was posted to 107 Squadron at Harwell on 1st December 1938 after being re-mustered as Wireless Operator on 16th November. John was then re-mustered as Wireless Operator/Air Crew on 29th January 1939 and Wireless Operator/Air Gunner on 1st March, reclassified as AC 1 on 1st November and again to Leading Aircraftsman on 1st February 1940. His last entry shows he was promoted to Sergeant on 27th May 1940 (the record having finally being brought up to date).

John's family were notified that he was posted missing on 29th May 1940. Receiving a letter from the Air Council dated 27th February 1941 stating that "due to lapse of time and the absence of any further news since he was

P.352477/40/P.4. Cas.

AIR MINISTRY
Dept. Q. J.

27 February, 1941.

Sir,

I am commanded by the Air Council to state that in view of the lapse of time and the absence of any further news regarding your son, 548565 Leading Aircraftman J. Mahoney, since the date on which he was reported missing, they must regretfully conclude that he has lost his life, and his death will be presumed, for official purposes, to have occurred on the 27th May, 1940.

The Council desire me to express again their sincere sympathy with you in your bereavement and in the anxiety which you have suffered.

I am, Sir,

Your obedient Servant,

Charles Evans

C. Mahoney Esq.,
78, Symmons Street,
Warren Weir,
Swansea,
Glam.

Letter to Mr. Mahoney

reported missing it will be presumed that his date of death, for official purposes will be 27th May 1940".

Another letter was received from the Air Council dated 10th December 1943, stating that a French organisation called Anciens Combattants reported that an "English Soldier" (as they called him) named Mahoney, number 548565 was buried in the commune of Marck, Pas de Calais. The Air Council also stated the proximity of this to the area that Harry and his crew were operating, and so were in no doubt that this information is correct.

AIR MINISTRY,

~~ADASTRAL HOUSE,~~

~~KINGSWAY, W.C.2~~

Casualty Branch

77, Oxford Street

London, W.1.

P.352477/40/P.4/108

16 IK December, 1943.

Dear Mr. Mahoney,

As long ago as 27th February, 1941, a letter was sent you on behalf of the Air Council saying that, in view of the lapse of time and the absence of news, it had been regretfully decided that your son, 548565 Leading Aircraftman (later Sergeant) J. Mahoney had lost his life, and that his death would be presumed to have occurred on 27th May, 1940.

Now, after a long delay, we have received some information about his fate. A French organisation known as the Anciens Combattants has reported that an "English soldier" (as they call him) called Mahoney, number 548565, is buried in the commune of Marck (Pas de Calais).

There can be no doubt that this is your son. His aircraft had been detailed to attack enemy motor transport on the St. Omer – La Payellette road, so that the area of operations and the position of the grave are fairly close. Marck lies about 20 miles north west and La Payellette 4 miles east-south-east of St. Omer.

I feel you would like to have this positive, though sadly belated, piece of information, and I pass it on to you in the hope that it may bring you a measure of consolation in your bereavement.

Yours sincerely,

G. Mahoney, Esq.,
78, Symmons Street,
Warren Weir,
Swansea,
Glamorgan.

A.P. le M. Swinson

(Flight Lieutenant in Casualty Branch)

A9 Air Ministry letter to Mr. Mahoney 10.12.43

This was not the end of the story. A letter dated 8th November 1947 gives more detail into the fate of John. The Royal Air Force Missing Research and Enquiry Services in France completed extensive investigations trying to establish what happened to missing Air Crew, one of these being John. This document followed on from the previous report where it had been confirmed that his aircraft had crashed in the sea off the coast of Calais in May 1940. His body had been washed ashore, and was identified by his service number. At the time

Air Ministry letter to Mr. Mahoney 18.11.47 (pages 1 and 2)

Tel. No.
SLOANE 3467 Ext............ ......

AIR MINISTRY,
2, SEVILLE STREET,
LONDON, S.W.I.

Ref. P.352477/40/S.14 Cas/C4.

8 November, 1947.

Dear Mr. Mahoney,

It is with great reluctance that I have to re-open the subject of the sad loss of your son, Sergeant John Mahoney, but I feel sure you will wish to know that the Royal Air Force Missing Research and Enquiry Services in France have recently completed their investigations concerning his fate.

It has been confirmed that your son's aircraft crashed in the sea off the coast of Calais and his body was washed ashore near Marck in May 1940, being identified by his service number "543565". At the time there were many bodies on the beaches and the Germans arrived and ordered the civilian authorities at Marck to bury them. The French authorities were given four hours to do this, but owing to the short time allowed it was impossible to transfer the bodies to a cemetery. Out of a total of sixty five men including Army personnel, only five could be identified one of whom was your son, and they were all buried in the sand dunes of Les Hemmes De Marck.

After two years of effort, the town officials of Marck finally obtained permission from the Germans to move the bodies from the beach to the cemetery of Les Hemmes. Of the sixty five bodies that were buried in 1940 only thirty nine could be found in 1942. The remainder had either been washed away by the sea or buried in shifting sand dunes.

C. Mahoney, Esq.,
78 Symmons Street,
Warren Weir,
Swansea, Glamorgan.

/Unhappily......

Unhappily the five who were originally buried in the sand dunes were never again found.

A further search was made in the Marck Communal Cemetery and exhumation of all British "unknown" buried there was undertaken, this again produced no result.

I much regret the distressing nature of this belated information and I hasten to extend my very sincere sympathy with you in the great loss you have sustained.

Yours sincerely,

D. Bent

there were many bodies on the beaches and, when they arrived, the Germans ordered the civilian authorities to bury them. Given only four hours to do this there wasn't time to move them to a cemetery. Out of sixty-five men, both RAF and Army personnel, only five could be identified, one of these being John. They were all buried in the sand dunes of Les Hemmes de Marck. Following two years of effort the French finally gained permission from the Germans to remove the bodies from the beach. Of the sixty-five bodies buried in 1940 only thirty-nine could be found in 1942, the remainder being either washed away by the sea or buried in shifting sand dunes. Unfortunately the five that had been identified in 1940 could not be found. In 1946/47 the RAF branch carried out exhumations of all unknown British personnel in the Marck Communal Cemetery, but again this proved inconclusive regarding what happened to John. John is commemorated on Panel 17 of the RAF Memorial at Runnymede.

CHAPTER ELEVEN

The German Pilots

Rudolf Goy

My research enabled me to find out the names of the German pilots who attacked Harry's plane.

LT Rudolf Goy had joined the Luftwaffe in the 1930s. In 1938 he was part of 3 Staffel Jagdgruppe 88 of the Legion Condor in Spain during the Spanish Civil War. Flying the Messerschmitt Bf109D, code 6-75, he shot down a Polikarpov I16 Rata to the east of Valencia on 19th July: the first of his combat victories. Again on 23rd September he destroyed two more I16 Ratas. On 1st May 1939, Rudolf was promoted to Oberleutnant and posted to Staka 1

Rudolf Goy in 1939

Jagdfliegervorschule 5. He was then posted as commander of 4/Jagdgeshwader 53 and then later as commander of 5/Jagdgeschwader 53. In combat at 17.05hrs on 30th September 1939 he was responsible for shooting down a Mureaux 115 French reconnaissance aircraft flying a Bf109D as RED 1. This action took place near Wissembourg.

With the invasion of the Low Countries the Staffel were in action on a daily basis. With the German ground forces getting a lot of attention from the Royal Air Force, the Luftwaffe were called upon to provide air cover. During 107 Squadron's attack on the woodland to the East of St Omer on 27th May 1940, Rudolf – flying by this time the better Bf109E4 – along with Eduard Berwanger and Artur Trutwin chased 107 Squadron out to sea. This is when Rudolf scored his fifth and final air victory shooting down Harry Warman, a shared claim with the other two pilots.

As the war progressed JG53 moved to a base at Charleville, and their pilots became heavily involved in the Battle of Britain.

Rudolf was promoted to Hauptman and posted to Staka1/JFS2 with the appointment of Gruppenleiter (group leader) on 10th September 1940, until being posted to JG54 on 1st December 1941. Another posting came on 9th February 1943 when he moved to Stab/Jagdfleigerfuhrer 3. He was promoted again on 1st April 1944, this time to Major. Out of nine veterans of the Spanish Civil War that served with JG53, Rudolf was one of only two to survive the Second World War. The other was Oberleutnant Pingel, who became a prisoner of war.

Rudolf was awarded the Spanish Cross and Iron Cross 1st and 2nd class along with a Fighter Operational Control Clasp.

Eduard Berwanger

Lt Eduard Berwanger was another veteran of the Spanish Civil War. Eduard, also serving with 5/JG53, shared the shooting down of Harry on 27th May. He went on to fight in the Battle of Britain.

On 13th August 1940 JG53 were in action over Portland, Dorset. During this combat he accounted for damaging a Spitfire, north of Portland. This aircraft was, most probably, Spitfire R6608 from 152 Squadron based at Warmwell. Records show that this plane was attacked while itself attacking a Messerschmitt 110. Pilot Officer R F Innes returned to base slightly wounded in the elbow but his aircraft was written off. Although the German records show that Eduard shot down two Spitfires it seems more likely that his second aircraft that day was a Hurricane. Shot down south of Portland, the only record that seems to tie in with this is Hurricane P3177 of 238 Squadron based at Middle Wallop. This plane was believed to have been shot down in combat over Portland at 16.30hrs; its pilot Sergeant H J Marsh was posted missing and the aircraft lost.

Eduard's run of luck ran out on 26th August when in combat over the English Channel he was attacked by Spitfires of 234 Squadron based at Middle Wallop. Eduard ditched in the sea off Cherbourg. One record shows that Eduard was believed to have been rescued by Seenotdienst (German Air Sea Rescue) and the aircraft lost. Although Kracker Luftwaffe Archive shows him as being killed in action. It may well be that he was rescued but died later. Eduard was awarded the Iron Cross 1st and 2nd Class with the Fighter Operational Control Clasp.

Artur Trutwin

Born in Essen on 25th October 1910. Artur joined the police force in April 1931. After this he went into the Luftwaffe, joining on 1st May 1935 and drafted to KG27, Geschwader Boelke. He began training as a pilot on 12th January 1938.

Oberfeldwebel Artur Trutwin served with 5/JG53 sharing the claim of Rudolf Goy and Eduard Berwanger. Artur was again heavily involved during the early stages of the Battle of Britain. During the same combat that Eduard shot down two aircraft, Artur, flying a Bf109E1, was to become a victim himself. He was attacked over the Channel off Weymouth and crashed into the sea. On 25th August an unidentified body was recovered from the sea. It was badly decomposed so the Town Clerk and a Medical Referee (Dr Gordon Wallace) decided the he should be cremated, for public health reasons. This took place at Weymouth Crematorium on 26th August. The only reference to the identity was an identity disc with the body giving the following details: BLGR/O, 67010/7. It was obviously not possible to do anything at the time, but subsequent investigation in 1947 revealed that this was the body of Artur Trutwin. His ashes were scattered in the gardens of remembrance with little fuss or religious ceremony.

Chapter Twelve

William Warman

William, the eldest son of George and Bessie Warman was born 15th November 1909, at 4 Fladbury Road, Tottenham, London, where his father was working at the time. By 1912 the family had moved to Mannings Heath, Sussex. William attended Mannings Heath School and

William in Royal Artillery

William and his half brother Les and 'Tiddler' with their mother Bessie

then went onto Lower Beeding School, on 10th September 1923. William then went to live with his mother in London. He was working as a glass blower until joining the army in 1930.

802087 Gunner William Warman enlisted in the Royal Artillery on 29th April 1930. He was posted to Depot Brigade on 1st May 1930 and then to the 3rd Training Battalion on the 10th. After completing his training he was posted to the 32nd Holding Battalion awaiting a posting to a regiment. A short posting to the 26/7th Medium Brigade was followed by a posting to Aden, with the 9th Heavy Battery. William stayed with the 9th until

18th February 1933 when he was posted to the 24th Heavy Battery, serving in Hong Kong. William arrived in Hong Kong on 17th March 1933, remaining there until 12th February 1936 when he was posted to the Depot Brigade for administrative purposes while travelling home to Britain.

On arrival on 17th March, William was posted to the 35th /2nd Field Brigade which was at Louisburg Barracks, Bordon, Hampshire. William received the appointment of Acting Lance Bombardier (unpaid) on 4th May 1937 and to Lance Bombardier (paid) on 13th February 1938. The 35th/2nd Field Brigade was re-designated to the 35th/87th Battery Field Regiment, which was equipped with the recently introduced 25-pounder gun.

It is while William was stationed at Bordon he married the 24-year-old Monica Patricia Doreen Hilton at the Roman Catholic Church of the Sacred Heart, Bordon, on 7th June 1938. Monica was working in the NAAFI at Louisburg Barracks. Monica sometimes known as Mona was born in Lancashire. The couple had no children and Monica did not re-marry after William's death. Monica died in 1970. William's witness was one of his army mates, Gunner J Lowery.

William was posted to the 3rd Anti-Aircraft Regiment on 24th February 1939 and joined the 21st Anti-Aircraft Battery on 26th March, serving in Malaya (Singapore). Promoted to Bombardier on 1st June and posted to the 11th Battery, A/A. While with the 11th Battery he was promoted to Lance Sergeant on 12th March 1940. William was posted on 30th November 1940 to the 5th Searchlight Regiment based at Fort Siloso on Blakang Mati (now Sentosa), Singapore. While there he was promoted to Acting Sergeant on 13th March 1941 and relinquished that rank and reverted back to Lance Sergeant on 9th November.

CHAPTER THIRTEEN

Malaya and Singapore

Threats of hostilities from Japan had been rising during the autumn of 1941. The British strongholds of the Far East were a target and a prize possession should Japan be able to take them. The events in Malaya and Singapore were in part an effect of the Japanese invasion of China and Korea. The governments of Britain, America and Holland placed embargoes on the supply of raw materials to Japan. Oil, iron and rubber were the main commodities affected by this. The French and the Dutch defeat in Europe paved the way for the Japanese to take control of French Indo-China (Vietnam) and the Dutch East Indies (Indonesia).

The British territory of Malaya was rich in the raw materials that Japan desperately needed. For Japan it was a logical move to try to capture this prize from the British who had relied on the rubber plantations of that region. Singapore, at the southern tip of the Malayan peninsula was a strategic point for Britain in providing an all-important naval base for the protection of her interests in the Far East and the trade routes to and from Australia and New Zealand.

The biggest threat to Japan was the large American Naval base at Pearl Harbour, Honolulu, Hawaii. The Japanese felt it was necessary to limit this threat so at 03.28hrs on 8th December 1941 Tokyo time (07.48hrs 7th December Hawaiian time; 18.18hrs GMT) the Japanese Navy launched its warplanes from aircraft carriers to attack

Pearl Harbour. Many of the US battleships were in harbour at the time of the surprise attack and severe damage was done. The Japanese also attacked the American airfields to prevent the Americans getting airborne to defend their battleships. The American aircraft carriers were at sea so they survived.

Japan declared war on the USA and Great Britain on 7th December 1941 (8th December Japanese time). At 02.15hrs (Tokyo time) the Japanese 25th Army's 18th Division landed at Kota Bahru, in the north east of Malaya, marking the start of the Malayan campaign. On 8th December the Battleships *HMS Prince of Wales* and *HMS Repulse* along with their destroyer escorts, had been sent from Singapore to search for signs of Japanese forces landing on the Malayan coast. On receiving a message that the fleet had been discovered by the Japanese, Admiral Sir Tom Phillips returned to Singapore.

While on the return voyage a signal came through about an invasion at Kuantan on Malaya's east coast. The fleet turned north again to try to intercept the invading forces. On the 10th one of the two Supermarine Walrus flying boats was catapult launched from *HMS Repulse* with Petty Officer William Crozer at the controls, to search for the invading forces and make an anti-submarine patrol. After finding nothing Crozer was returning to *Repulse* when he saw the fleet under attack from Japanese dive bombers. On the first attack only minor damage was done, but then the Japanese sent in more aircraft, this time armed with torpedoes. Within a short time both of the battleships had been sunk with the loss of over 800 seamen. This led to the situation being perilous for the land forces.

Lt Gen A E Percival, Officer Commanding, Malaya had at his disposal about 80,000 troops dispersed over the whole peninsula. The troops consisted of British,

Australian and Indian (for ease referred to as British). The fighter element of the Royal Air Force was 150 obsolete Brewster Buffalos and a handful of Hawker Hurricanes. While the bomber force consisted of 62, 60 and 27 Squadrons operating from bases in northern Malaya and 34 Squadron based at Tengah, Singapore. 60 and 62 Squadrons were operating the Bristol Blenheim Mk I, 27 Squadron had a mix of Blenheim Mk I bombers and Mk I (F) fighters while 34 Squadron was equipped with the Blenheim Mk IV. This gave a total of forty-seven aircraft with fifteen in reserve. These squadrons suffered badly from enemy action along with a shortage of spares. A small number of replacement aircraft arrived but not enough to make a difference.

By Christmas 1941 the squadrons re-grouped at Tengah with a total of nineteen Mk IV and five Mk I and Mk I (F). By the end of January 1942 the remaining aircraft were withdrawn to Sumatra. Percival had no tanks as it was felt they would be of no use in jungle fighting. Soon after the landing at Kota Bahru Japanese bombers attacked the naval base and Keppel Harbour docks and the airbases at Tengah and Seletar, Singapore. When considering what Percival had at his disposal it needs to be understood that with the war in Europe and Africa – added to the fact that Singapore is so far away – it was difficult for Britain to send enough stocks out to the Far East. Although much closer to India, the British forces there were themselves suffering from a lack of equipment due to the war in Europe and Africa, and so were not in a position to provide much additional support for Singapore.

The Japanese army pushed forward through Malaya driving the British troops towards Singapore. On 31st January 1942 the British troops crossed over into Singapore. Once over it, the causeway between Malaya and Singapore was blown up and partly destroyed by the

British only for it to be repaired by the Japanese by 11th February.

It appears that Lt Gen Percival might have fallen into the same trap that his commanding officer had fallen into during the Battle of the Somme in 1916 when he had tried to pass on advice from the officers on the ground and had been ignored. On this occasion it was Percival who was ignoring the advice. He was being advised by his engineering officers that he would need to strengthen his northern defences, and did not act on it. It has to be taken into account that Percival had limited resources. The defences on the northern coast of Singapore were weak as it was always thought that any invasion would be from the south. Heavy artillery was placed around the east and the south of the island. To the east were two batteries of guns on Pulau Tekong consisting of Tekong battery with three 9.2inch guns and Sphinx with two 6inch guns. On the east of the mainland at Changi were three batteries, one with three 15inch guns and two batteries with two 6inch guns. To the west was one battery of two 6inch guns and on the mainland in the south Buona Vista battery had two 15inch guns and Labrador had two 6inch guns. The three forts on Blakang Mati, Serapong, Connaught and Siloso were armed with two 6inch guns each at Serapong and Siloso and three 9.2inch guns at Connaught. These forts also had a good establishment of anti-aircraft artillery. It was here that William was stationed as part of the searchlight defences.

Anticipating that the threat would come from the south these deliberately under-strength defences proved to be of no major use. The invasion of the island took place to the north which was defended only by infantry with light artillery support. The infantry consisted of the British 18th Division, the Indian 9th and 11th Divisions and the Australian Imperial Forces with the untrained Indian 44th Brigade attached to them.

The Japanese invasion started on 7th February when a diversionary attack was made on Palau Ubin by 400 troops of Japanese Imperial Guards. Resistance was light and this small island to the east of the mainland was taken easily. The main attack took place at Sarimbun on the 8th and Kranji on the 9th. The Japanese 18th Division's first wave met stiff resistance from the Australian defences but these were heavily outnumbered and with subsequent waves of enemy coming ashore and ammunition running short the Australians had no choice but to retreat. The Japanese drove a wedge down the centre of Singapore so Lt Gen Percival had to bring in his other forces to counter the threat. Struggling with poor communications and ammunition running low, the defenders were increasingly disadvantaged as more Japanese troops arrived.

On the 14th the remaining aircraft of the RAF element in Singapore were evacuated to Java. On the morning of the 15th Percival held a meeting of his senior staff to discuss the situation which was becoming impossible. Having little choice, with his supplies running low and very little chance should a counter attack take place, surrender was the only realistic option. The surrender of Singapore took place at the Ford Motor Factory – the headquarters of Lt Gen Yamashita – at 18.10hrs local time on 15th February.

The roundup of prisoners was very swift. William was officially posted missing on 15th February 1942. He and the other defenders of Fort Siloso remained there as prisoners for a while before they were taken to the Malayan Prisoner of War camp at Changi. William's prisoner number was 8,505. Changi Prison Complex, Singapore had been built some years earlier by the British as a civilian prison. As a POW camp Changi became notorious for being extremely overcrowded, and for the harsh treatment of its prisoners who received

收容所 Camp	馬來	
姓名 Name	Warman, William.	昭和　　年　　月　　日
國籍 Nationality	英	番號 No.	5.505
階級身分 Rank	SERGEANT 軍曹	生年月日 Date of Birth	15TH NOVEMBER 1909
捕獲場所 Place of Capture	SINGAPORE 昭南	所屬部隊 Unit	No. 602047, 5TH SEARCHLIGHT REGT. RA ARMY.
父ノ名 Father's Name	JOSEPH RICHARDSON (STEP FATHER).	捕獲年月日 Date of Capture	昭和 17 年 2 月 15 日
本籍地 Place of Origin	HORSHAM, SUSSEX ENGLAND.	母ノ名 Mother's Name	BESSIE RICHARDSON
通報先 Destination of Report	WIFE: MONICA PATRICIA DORINE WARMAN 1 ALMA COTTAGE DEADWATER HILL, BORDEN, HAMPSHIRE ENGLAND.	職業 Occupation	GLASS BLOWER.
		特記事項 Remarks	

William's Japanese PoW Record Card
Copyright National Archives

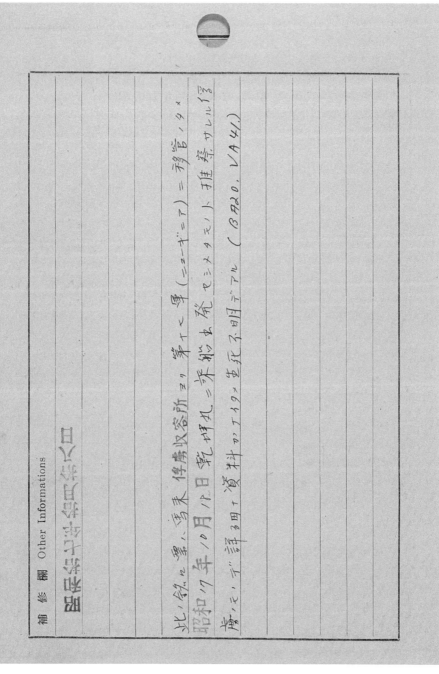

昭和拾七年拾月拾八日補修

此ノ例ハ鑑ニ寫真添付捕虜収容所ヨリ第十八軍（ニューギニア）ニ移管、昭和17年10月18日乾坤丸ニ乗船ヲ発セシメタルト推察サレル13名デアル

考ニ、テ、評3冊ト資料ガ、フィダヲ生死不明デアル（BA20. VA41.）

Translation

"This is a prisoner's ID. This person has probably been transferred from a prisoner of war camp on the Malay Peninsula to the Japanese Army military base (17 Regiment) in Papua New Guinea. He transferred by the *Kenkon Maru* (name of ship). However, there is no detail, or data, for this person. It is not clear if he is alive or dead."

Translated by Momoko Matsuo-Grover.

very little food and constant beatings. Later, in May of 1944 it was estimated that that around 12,000 prisoners were kept here. Another of the notorious prisons was the Selerang Barracks. Originally built to house 1,200 men, the Japanese crammed in as many as 15,400.

Conditions in the camps were exceedingly poor; there was a desperate lack of sanitation for so many prisoners and a dire lack of food. Disease took hold very quickly in the camps and many soon died of this or starvation. The civilians fared no better than the military prisoners. Many of the Chinese population were taken by their captors and brutally murdered. A large number of the military prisoners were taken from Singapore to other occupied territories to build railways, the most notorious of these being the Burma Railway. Others were taken – as in the case of the 600 Gunners Party – to build airfields. A number of others were taken to Japan, some of these later witnessing the bombing of Hiroshima and Nagasaki.

As the war progressed and the allies closed in on Japan, supplies became scarce and the meagre rations prisoners were given were cut still further. The Americans were bombing the Japanese mainland and bombers were also seen over Singapore, bombing the Seletar air base and the harbour.

Operation Zipper – the plan for the landings on Singapore by the allies – was planned for 6th August 1945 but this did not take place as the Americans dropped the atomic bombs on Hiroshima and Nagasaki leading to the surrender of Japan on 15th August. Two weeks later British troops returned to Singapore and on 12th September Lord Louis Mountbatten, Supreme Commander Allied Forces, accepted the surrender of all Japanese forces in South East Asia.

CHAPTER FOURTEEN

Ballale

The 600 Gunners Party

In early October 1942 the Japanese were in need of working parties. It was decided to take some of the prisoners from Singapore to do this work. 156 officers and 472 men from the Royal Artillery were taken for this. The unit comprised men from the:

35th Light Anti-Aircraft Regiment,

7th Coastal Regiment,

9th Coastal Regiment,

11th Coastal Regiment,

2nd and 3rd Heavy Anti-Aircraft Regiments,

5th Searchlight Regiment,

Singapore and Hong Kong Artillery

and the attached Royal Army Medical Corps and Royal Army Service Corps personnel.

Under the Command of Lt. Col J Bassett the unit were taken to Singapore docks where they boarded the *Kenkon Maru*. Some of the men suffered terribly from illness on the voyage, and it is thought that a couple may have died. The first stop was at Rabaul, New Britain. Under the tropical sun the men were worked hard, with very little food for nearly a month. Again many suffered from illness. With eighty-two deemed not fit enough for the work ahead, the remainder were again ordered onto the ship to be taken to Ballale Island where the Japanese Navy were building an airstrip.

Conditions were extremely bad on the ship. It was a two-day voyage so when they did arrive some of the men were not fit for work. While the airstrip was under construction it was of interest to the allied bombers; not knowing these men were on the island some were killed in the bombing raids. Others died of illness and some reports state that these were tied up in rice sacks and dumped at sea. It is not entirely clear but it seems that when the airstrip was finished and with the allies closing in on the area the Japanese had no use for the prisoners any more. It appears that the prisoners that were left – it is not known how many – were machine-gunned by their guards on or about 5th March 1943.

In November 1945 the Australian Army discovered a mass grave of fifty-seven bodies, all of these identified as prisoners of war but not identified individually. Another search of the island revealed another mass grave containing 438 bodies. Items found with the bodies proved that they were from the Royal Artillery. The bodies from these two mass graves were removed to the Bomana War Cemetery, Port Moresby, Papua New Guinea. Twenty-two bodies have never been found.

William was one of this party of gunners taken to Ballale as was Gunner 872289 John Lowery of the 9th Coastal Regiment, Royal Artillery. John was the witness at William's wedding. Lt Col Bassett was also among these.

Of the eighty-two men that did not travel to Ballale only eighteen survived, returning home to Britain. Within twelve years all of these had died, such was their treatment while in captivity.

BALLALE

CERTIFIED COPY OF   ENTRY OF DEATH

SAW 041488

Application Number 9078632-1

Registration of Births, Deaths and Marriages (Special Provisions) Act 1957

Return of Warrant Officers, Non-Commissioned Officers and Men of the Royal Regiment of Artillery Killed in Action or who have died whilst on Service Abroad between 3rd September 1939 and 30th June 1948 inclusive

Rgtl. or Army number	Rank	Name in Full (Surname First)	Age	Country of Birth	Date of Death	Place of Death	Cause of Death
802087	L/Sgt.	WARMAN William	32	England	on or shortly after 5.3.1943	Unknown Far East	Unknown whilst Prisoner of War Jap. Hands.

An Entry relating to the death of William Warman

CERTIFIED to be a true copy of the certified copy of* an entry in a Service Departments Register.

Given at the General Register office, under the seal of the said Office, the 27th day of March 2018

Section 3(2) of the above mentioned Act provides that "The enactments relating to the registration of births and deaths and marriages in England and Wales, Scotland and Northern Ireland (which contain provisions authorising the admission in evidence of, and of extracts from, certified copies of registers and duplicate registers) shall have effect as if the Service Departments Registers were certified copies or duplicate registers transmitted to the Registrar General in accordance with those enactments."

CAUTION: THERE ARE OFFENCES RELATING TO FALSIFYING OR ALTERING A CERTIFICATE AND USING OR POSSESSING A FALSE CERTIFICATE. © Crown Copyright

*If the certificate is given from the original Register the words 'the certified copy of' are struck out.

WARNING: A CERTIFICATE IS NOT EVIDENCE OF IDENTITY

734137SI SI2674 04/15 WL/A1TPS

William's Death Certificate

83

All these men are commemorated on the Singapore War Memorial at Kranji. Bringing this story up to date, I had the good fortune to go to Singapore with a group of ten Army Cadets and another instructor from Sussex in November 2017. We held a short wreath-laying ceremony at Kranji. The Singaporeans kindly changed our programme to allow us to do this. It was a special occasion as we had twenty Indian Cadets and three instructors; ten American Cadets and one instructor; ten Australian Cadets and three instructors with an Australian Colonel who was visiting; four Brunei Cadets and two Instructors along with a number of Cadets and instructors from the Singapore National Cadet Corps.

CHAPTER FIFTEEN

Other Lives

Although focusing on Harry and William Warman, my research touched on a number of other lives. This chapter tells some of their stories.

George Warman

George, the middle brother of William and Harry, was born on 29th November 1912. He attended Mannings Heath School, Sussex before moving to Lower Beeding School with William. George moved in with his Uncle and the family at Southwater in 1924 and took the entrance exam for the Royal Hospital School, which was at Greenwich at the time, but is now at Holbrook, Suffolk. This school was for the sons of ex Royal Navy sailors.

On leaving school George worked in shop-fitting and the building industry, which took him around the country. George settled in Bedford. He married Edith May Morgan on 3rd December 1938. George and Edith's daughter, Julie was born on 19th August 1939.

On the outbreak of war he was building air raid shelters and so was exempt from service. Later in the war George received his call up papers. 14593159 Private George Warman joined the army on 6th May 1943 and reported for duty with the Kings Own Scottish Borderers on 21st June. George was not called upon to go overseas and was released from the army on Category B to the reserve and discharged on 29th March 1945. (MOD CS(R) 2B, Ref

93/85664/3/ 4/1/94). As he had been in the building trade before the war, there was a need for tradesmen with these skills to start on the repair and re-building of bomb damaged buildings now the war was ending.

Harry Jones

The death of Harry Jones of Lorna Doone, Worthing Road, Horsham, (now part of Southwater) was reported in the *West Sussex County Times* on 20th October 1939. Harry was the first Horsham war casualty of the Second World War.

Harry was the second child of Harry and Florence Jones, born in 1923. One of the cousins of Harry Warman, he was at Victory Road School in Horsham before going to St John's School. While at school Harry had been quite a sportsman, becoming the Sussex Schools High Jump Champion in 1936. He was also quite artistic, and had some talent at drawing and sketching.

Harry joined the Royal Navy as a Boy Seaman on 8th February 1937 after working at a local shop for a year. He did his training at St Vincent Training Establishment, Gosport. Harry worked hard during his training, and was promoted to Leading Boy and then to Petty Officer Instructor Boy. At this rank Harry spent longer than normal at St Vincent. During his time in training he was a member of the Field Gun Crew in the winter term of 1938. While he was with the team they set a new record of 1 min and 24 secs.

On leaving St Vincent Harry was posted to *HMS Royal Oak* which was based in Scapa Flow. *HMS Royal Oak* was an old ship by this time, and was slow compared to most of the ships of the day. Launched in 1914 and completed in 1916, she took part in the Battle of Jutland in 1916. On 14th October 1939 the German U47 commanded by

HMS Royal Oak

Lieutenant Gunther Prien broke into Scapa Flow and torpedoed the *Royal Oak*. The ship went down soon after with the loss of 833 out of the crew of 1,234, some of these casualties dying of wounds after the sinking.

P/JX Boy 1st Class Harry was only sixteen at the time; a few days later he would have been seventeen. Harry was not the only one from Horsham involved in the sinking, the other was Peter Boyce. One of Harry's colleagues from training, Arthur Merritt from Slinfold, Sussex had just sailed from Scapa Flow that day. Harry is commemorated on Panel 34 Column 2 of the Portsmouth Naval Memorial.

Harry Jones, Royal Navy

Gunther Prien became a hero in Germany after this exploit, and was paraded through the streets of Berlin where he met Adolf Hitler.

With the wreck being a War Grave, the *Royal Oak* was placed under the protection of the Protection of Military Remains Act 1986.

May Jones

Harry Warman's cousin May (sister to Harry Jones) worked in the Women's Land Army. She was working in the dairy at South Lodge, Lower Beeding. South Lodge estate had a fairly large dairy at Peppers Gate Farm, and milk from their own herds was bottled and delivered from there. Percy Powell was the delivery man.

May was lodging with Mrs Parsons (a widow) and her daughter Betty next door to the farm. It is not known when May started working there but she was working there in 1944 as she appears in the photograph of the staff of South Lodge taken with them wearing their relevant uniforms. South

May Jones in 1944

Lodge was one of the main large estates in the area, belonging to the Godman family.

Les Richardson

Harry's half- brother, 1291764 LAC Les Richardson trained at Blackpool as a Wireless Operator in the Royal Air Force. He went to Rhodesia in 1941 as part of the Empire Training Schools and was discharged at Salisbury, Rhodesia at the end of the war. He married Doreen who was also a wireless operator in the RAF.

George Warman Snr

George was born on 22nd January 1879. He joined the Royal Navy as a Boy Rating on 19th February 1894 at Portsmouth. On entering adult service in 1897, 178236 Ordinary Seaman George Warman signed on for twelve years' service. After a rather uneventful career in respect that the Royal Navy did not carry out much in the way of operations, he came out of the Navy in on 22nd January 1909. He was recommended for the Royal Fleet Reserve.

On the outbreak of the First World War he re-joined the Navy on 2nd August 1914; his occupation was listed then as Wireman (telegraph). It is known from a postcard he sent back home to George junior that he was in Bermuda at some point in 1916. He was discharged in October 1919.

Miss Elizabeth May Oakey

Although others in this chapter are of interest from a services point of view I felt it important to include May Oakey in this section. May, the daughter of Frederick and Hannah Oakey was born on 14th August 1895 in Fulham. At the time of the 1901 census May's father was listed as a conductor on stage coaches and they were living at 70 Hartismere Road, Fulham.

In 1911 they were living at 41 Santos Road, Wandsworth. May's father by this time was a driver of motor buses. He worked for London Transport, retiring on 14th July 1934 after forty-one years of service. May by this time had qualified as a teacher and became the Headmistress at Lower Beeding in 1924. A lot of the pupils regarded her as a bit of a dragon, but I think she was a fair person. May was a smoker and it would be frowned on by today's standards, but she used to give cigarettes to the lads that smoked. Some of her teaching methods were a little ahead of the time. May encouraged her pupils in drama. School plays were a regular occurrence. The pupils also attended drama events at Lodge Hill, near Pulborough. In the 1939 register it shows that May had her retired parents living with her at Lower Beeding.

After retirement May bought the old School House (which she re-named Penlee) when the old Lower Beeding School closed in July of 1966. May continued to give extra tuition to a number of children long after her retirement. In about 1980 she went into St Leonards Park Nursing home just outside Horsham, and at this time I lost touch with her. May died on 14th July 1984.

CHAPTER SIXTEEN

107 Squadron

No 107 Squadron was formed as part of the Royal Flying Corps at Lake Down, Salisbury, on 8th May 1918. Flying the DH9 Bomber the squadron moved to the Western Front in June. In action from the 30th June when seven aircraft bombed Menin Railway station, they were constantly active bombing enemy targets until the Armistice. Their last raid was on 9th November 1918 two days before the ceasefire.

At one point during this time in France the squadron was attached to the French Army. Carrying out many successful missions, the squadron dropped nearly forty tons of bombs and claimed sixteen enemy aircraft downed.

With the war over and the inevitable cuts that took place, 107 Squadron was disbanded in 1919.

At Upavon on 10th August 1936, the squadron was reformed with Hawker Hinds to carry out a bomber role once more. A move to Old Sarum in February 1937 followed, lasting until June when they moved again, this time to Harwell. It was while the squadron was at Harwell that HM King George VI visited and approved the squadron badge: a double headed eagle with a collar of fleur de lys. The motto was *'Nous y Serons'*, translated as, 'We shall be there'.

107 exchanged its Hawker Hinds for the Bristol Blenheim Mk I in August 1938. During this period training was

Squadron badge
Reproduced by
permission of the
Ministry of Defence
with acknowledgement
to the Royal Air Force
Heraldry Trust and artist
Mary Denton

being stepped up considerably with the prospect of war looming once more. Ten months later the Mk Is were changed for the Blenheim Mk IV which they used until January 1942 when they took on the Douglas Boston. This, in turn, was changed for the de Havilland Mosquito in February of 1944. The Mosquito was to stay with the squadron until October 1948 when the squadron was based in Germany and renumbered to 11 Squadron. Many notable raids were undertaken by the squadron throughout the war, with a short spell with coastal command and a detachment to Malta. The squadron had many different bases during this period. The squadron was coded BZ from the Munich crisis until the outbreak of war when it received the code OM which it kept until 1948.

CHAPTER SEVENTEEN

Basil Embry

I felt it fitting to include a small chapter on Basil Embry as he was a great source of inspiration to his pilots and crews.

Basil Embry joined the Royal Air Force in 1931, taking his first flight at Netheravon on 5th April in an Avro 504K. On 26th April he had to make a forced landing due to an engine failure. On completion of his training at Netheravon in 1922 he was appointed to No 4 Squadron at Farnborough, with an attachment to the Armament and Gunnery School at Eastchurch for a three-month course on bombing and gunnery. Embry put in an application to serve overseas and in July he was notified that he had been selected to serve in Iraq. Before he could go there, he had to go on a conversion course to fly twin-engine aircraft.

Once this was finished he left Southampton on the Royal Air Force troopship *Braemar Castle* for Iraq. He reached Baghdad in October for the start of a three-year tour with 45 Squadron. He flew the Vickers Vernon until applying for a new posting which saw him moving to 70 Squadron in 1925. With 70 he was flying the DH9A – an aircraft that was designed as a bomber during the First World War. These postings gave him a lot of valuable experience in long-range flights which were to prove useful in years to come. He moved back home in 1927 to go on training duties.

He next joined the Central Flying School at Upavon where he stayed until being posted to India at the end of 1933, taking up a Staff appointment at Headquarters – a job he enjoyed doing but that did not give him the opportunity to fly. His chance to fly again came when, after being promoted to Squadron Leader, he took command of 20 Squadron on the North West Frontier.

In 1939 Embry returned to Britain. The RAF had changed considerably in the few years he had been away. There had been a huge expansion programme in the 30s, and aircraft had moved on, whereas he had been flying obsolete types overseas. On his promotion to Wing Commander he was posted to command 21 Squadron at Watton. He hadn't been in post long before he was sent on a conversion course to fly the Bristol Blenheim, which led to him being posted to command 107 Squadron on 14th September 1939.

The early part of the war was mainly anti-shipping work until the German invasion of Norway. This was to involve Bomber Command operating over hostile territory, which showed up the operational and tactical shortcomings of the RAF. This led Embry to question many things. He was instrumental in getting air crew promoted to the minimum rank of sergeant so they would be in the same messes to build up the team work required. He devised a new defensive armament for the Blenheim which he put into practice by getting his engineers to devise and fit.

At certain times he clashed with authority, but he always led from the front, earning great respect from his men. During the winter months the crews would get wet going to their aircraft which when flying in intense cold reduced the efficiency of the crews so he insisted that they should be taken to the aircraft.

With some of these measures in place it gave a much stronger platform to fight the enemy when they invaded the Low Countries in May 1940. During this period the squadron operated almost daily and sometimes twice a day. Embry was promoted to Group Captain on the morning of 27th May with a posting to command West Raynham. He was due to leave Wattisham at 16.00hrs but all this changed when a message came in from Group HQ for a raid that evening.

By arrangement with W/Cdr Stokes, the new squadron commander, he was to lead one last mission with the squadron. This was to prove more eventful than he thought. He was shot down over the target. He was taken prisoner but managed to escape, was captured again and escaped a second time. After being captured and escaping a third time, he managed to get through France and arrived back at base on 2nd August 1940. The full story of Embry's escape can be found in *Wingless Victory* by Anthony Richardson.

A number of postings followed during the war, with him still undertaking some unofficial operational flying.

Post war he had postings in Whitehall and after three years there was appointed as C in C Fighter Command at the rank of Air Chief Marshall. While at Fighter Command he undertook some major restructuring. On leaving Fighter Command he was posted to NATO which he found extremely frustrating and left the RAF in 1956.

For further reading please see: *Mission Completed* by Basil Embry.

CHAPTER EIGHTEEN

Memorials

Harry Warman For a number of years I attended **Lower Beeding Church** on Remembrance Sunday and Harry's name was always read out in the Roll of Honour. His name is on the plaque inside the church. Harry is also commemorated on the Roll of honour at Collyer's School, Horsham.

The **Royal Air Force Memorial**, Runnymede commemorates those Airman of the Air Forces of the Commonwealth who lost their lives while serving from bases in the UK, Iceland and the Faroe Isles, Northern Ireland, the Azores and bases on the continent of Europe who have no known grave.

Harry is commemorated on panel 20.

William Paish is on panel 18.

John Mahoney is on panel 17.

There is a memorial to 2 Group Bomber Command in **Ely Cathedral** and this commemorates all those of 2 Group who lost their lives.

St Clement Danes Church, The Strand, London. This is the Central Church of the Royal Air Force and contains memorials to all who served including the Squadron Badges set into the floor.

The **Bomber Command Memorial** in Green Park, London.

Blazon: An Eagle wings displayed Sable perched on a demi-Ship Or.
Link: The demi-ship comes from the Arms of Ipswich to which the station is affiliated whilst the eagle alludes to RAF operations.
Date of Issue: August 1940
Motto: Latin: Supra mare supra terramque - Above the sea and above the land

RAF Station Wattisham opened on 3 April 1939 and transferred to Army control on 1 July 1993

Commissioned by Mr David Parker in Memory of Sgt. Harry Warman of 107 Sqn whose Blenheim was shot down flying from RAF Wattisham on the raid against St. Omer, 27 May 1940.

RAF Wattisham badge
Reproduced by permission of the Ministry of Defence with
acknowledgement to the Royal Air Force Heraldry Trust
and artist Mary Denton

During the preparation of this book I felt I would set up a personal memorial to Harry. The means to do this came with the formation of the Royal Air Force Heraldry Trust whose aim was to provide a permanent record of all RAF badges, from Squadrons, RAF Stations and Maintenance Units. Sponsorship was being sought for the completion of this vast project. I was unable to sponsor the 107 Squadron Badge so I chose to sponsor RAF Wattisham instead, as this was the base Harry was flying from. This is dedicated to Harry.

There is a memorial to all those killed flying from RAF Wattisham at the Wattisham Station Heritage Museum inside the base. Visits by appointment only.

Lance Sergeant William Warman commemorated at the
Singapore War Memorial

William Warman

The **Singapore War Memorial**, Kranji, Singapore.
William Warman is commemorated here on panel 7.

Harry Jones

Horsham War Memorial

Portsmouth Naval Memorial, Panel 34. Column 2.

The Memorial Stone, Kranji

CHAPTER NINETEEN

On Reflection

With the story of two men it is surprising how much effect their loss had on others. The loss of their cousin, Harry's crew and ultimately the demise of two out of the three German pilots, would have had the same effect on their families. I use this as a mark of respect to them although at the time they were enemies; they shared the same fate and are now equal in death.

At a time of little opportunity for many, with Britain having suffered in the depression of the 1920s, Harry was lucky enough to go on to grammar school. This gave him a head start in the workplace when he left school. After two jobs with totally different companies which obviously didn't suit him he followed his sense of adventure and joined the Royal Air Force at a time of massive expansion. The Royal Air Force was transitioning from bi-planes to monoplanes; the aircraft were getting bigger; new aircraft types were being developed with greater speeds and ranges – the Bristol Blenheim being one of these. Although newer and faster than the contemporary fighters of the day when it was first designed and tested, the Blenheim had become obsolete by the outbreak of war in 1939.

In the early months of the Second World the RAF were mainly used for anti-shipping raids and reconnaissance, but this was soon to change when Germany invaded Norway in April 1940. It was the medium bombers of Bomber Command that took the brunt of the action. The

Norway Campaign was to be a short-lived action. The RAF faced the problems of the distance involved, flying over the North Sea. The weather was to play a huge part in in the viability of these operations. Aircraft frequently iced up at altitude; snow covered the targets and the crews suffered with severe cold. Events moved rapidly which led to the confusion regarding George thinking Harry had been shot down over Norway.

When 107 Squadron moved back to Wattisham from Lossiemouth at the beginning of May 1940 they had a short time to train and prepare for the onslaught that lay ahead. A number of Royal Air Force squadrons had been based in France for a few months, some of these being the light bomber squadrons with the Fairey Battle which proved to be slow and vulnerable to the German fighters. Alongside the Fairey Battles were some Blenheim squadrons. The fighter element was Gloster Gladiators and Hawker Hurricanes. The invasion and rapid advance of the German forces into Belgium and France meant that the home-based squadrons were soon in action. These faced heavy opposition from anti-aircraft fire from the guns supporting the German army and from the fighters of the Luftwaffe. Losses were heavy and damage to aircraft severe. With commanders like Basil Embry the RAF had good strong professional leaders, many of whom had seen service in far-flung corners of the Empire – the experience gained being invaluable. It has to be taken into account that these men were leading professional airmen. By the end of the war a vast number of these pre-war flyers had been killed, wounded or taken prisoner.

With the Battle of France closing – by which time Harry had been killed – the Luftwaffe concentrated on Britain with a view to dominate the skies in preparation for an invasion. The Battle of Britain started with hard-fought battles taking place over the southern counties. The focus for the RAF had now shifted from Bomber Command to Fighter Command. The German bombers, escorted by large numbers of fighters, concentrated on bombing airfields. The pilots of the Luftwaffe at this time consisted of many that had seen action during the Spanish Civil War, Rudolf Goy and Eduard Berwanger being just two of these. Although he had not seen action in Spain Artur Trutwin was a professional pilot at the outbreak of war. The Luftwaffe were on the back foot during the Battle of Britain from the point of view that the fighters were at the extreme of their range and could spend limited time over Britain. Added to this, any pilot shot down or those that bailed out would be taken prisoner apart from those killed. As for those that were wounded or flying damaged aircraft, they had to try to get back over the English Channel. As happened in the case of Eduard Berwanger he crashed into the sea and was picked up by the German Air Sea rescue.

The Far East campaigns have been largely overlooked by many people. I found myself guilty of this when I started to find out about William. I knew very little about the subject. It also seems that the fighting in Burma rather overshadows this war. Malaya and Singapore proved to be a hard blow to the British Empire. With the war by this time being conducted over Europe by the RAF there was a greater need for aircraft to enable them to keep up the offensive. Aircraft and ground forces were also heavily involved in the North Africa campaign so there was little to spare to reinforce the outposts of the Empire. I have spoken to some people I know who said their fathers were due to go to Singapore but were diverted to North Africa and some to Malta. These servicemen would quite likely have arrived in Singapore and gone into captivity soon after. A couple of convoys did arrive in Singapore with some Hawker Hurricanes but this was too little, and too late. Although William ended up on

Ballale Island many other prisoners were taken from Singapore to a number of other countries. The one everyone knows about is building of the Thai–Burma Railway. It was not just British and Empire troops used for these building projects; on Ballale a vast number of Koreans were in a camp near the British. Many of the personnel from Fort Siloso ended up being taken to Thailand or Japan. One incident that was not acknowledged by the British authorities for many years was that some of the Ballale 600 were on a ship bound for Japan when it was sunk by the Americans. Though they would not have known that the ship contained British prisoners, for many years the truth about the Ballale incident was kept covered up.

It was by good fortune that I had the opportunity to visit Singapore in November 2017. Coincidentally we flew out of Gatwick on 15th November, the date of William's birth. Before the visit I had planned to lay a wreath for William at the Singapore War Memorial. It was only intended to be a low key affair with just twelve of us, although this had been cleared through the High Commission. Fiona from the Singapore National Cadet Corps changed the training programme for me when I said what I would like to do. My low key event ended up with thirteen Australians, twenty-three Indians, eleven Americans and six from Brunei along with a group of Singaporeans – about eighty of us in total. For this I feel a great thank you is deserved to Fiona for making it better than I expected. Julie, William's niece found it hard to believe that so many should be there to honour her uncle.

With the story of Harry Jones and the sinking of *HMS Royal Oak* it was highlighted that there were 163 boy sailors on board of which, including Harry, 126 perished. After this incident it was accepted that boy sailors under eighteen years of age should not be serving on warships.

HMS Royal Oak was a veteran of the Battle of Jutland in 1916. She was outdated and had undergone extensive refits which had resulted in her being heavier and slower. In the summer of 1939 she was to be deployed to the Mediterranean, but this was cancelled due to the anticipated outbreak of war. Scapa Flow, the main base for the Royal Navy was considered to be safe from attack with block ships sunk across the entrances and booms stretched out to prevent U Boats entering. Up-to-date reconnaissance photographs showing the block ships and the number of ships moored in Scapa Flow allowed the U Boat commander, Gunter Prien to find the weak points to gain entry. By the time of the attack a number of the ships had put to sea, leaving fewer targets. Having selected *Royal Oak*, torpedoes were fired at her at 01.00hrs on 14th October one of these finding its target. A further three stuck home at 01.16hrs causing extensive damage and explosions. A couple of conspiracy theories surround this incident as they do in many cases and as Scapa Flow was deemed to be a safe haven it was not thought possible that a U Boat would be able to get in unaided. Legend had it that a German spy actually went out and guided Prien into the natural harbour. Another theory was that a German national living in Kirkwall planted a bomb in the magazines. Examination of the damage to *Royal Oak* disproves this.

The fate of U47, Prien's U Boat is not exactly known but the last radio message was on 7th March 1941 when it was near the Rockall Banks in the North Atlantic. It is known that *HMS Wolverine* was engaging a submarine in this area at the time so it is likely that this was U47.

I have mentioned earlier that Harry is commemorated on the Royal Navy Memorial, Portsmouth and the Horsham War Memorial, but he was not included on the Horsham War Memorial until the 1990s due to boundary changes. His home at the time was in Worthing Road,

Horsham but this became Worthing Road, Southwater. Another twist of fate came in 1940 when Victory Road School in Horsham burnt down. Harry's mother worked there and this was the school that Harry attended. In the remains of the burnt debris was a photograph of Harry, untouched by the fire but soaked with the water used to extinguish the fire. This led to Mrs Jones being convinced, up until her death that he had drowned and not burnt to death.

My aim was to convey the complexities of a small aspect of the Second World War and how those mentioned in the book played their part however large or small.

It just goes to show how far you can go from being given a Royal Air Force mess tunic and a love of history. I very much doubt this is the whole story as with any project of this nature there is bound to be something I have overlooked or not found yet.

I would be grateful if any reader has anything to add to the stories of the service personnel mentioned, if so could they please contact the publishers.

Bibliography

Aces of the Legion Condor, Robert Forsyth, Osprey Aircraft of the Aces, Osprey Publishing, 2011.

Aeroplane Magazine, Key Publishing. Various editions.

Attack Warning Red, Derek Wood, Macdonald and Jane's Publishers Ltd, 1976.

Blenheim Odyssey, Len Fearnley, Private Publication, 1989.

Blenheim Squadrons of World War 2, Jon Lake, Osprey Combat Aircraft. 5, Osprey Publishing, 1998.

Bristol Blenheim, Theo Boiten, Crowood Aviation Series, 1998.

Collyer's Casualties in Two World Wars, 1914-1918, 1939-1945. Garry Cooper. Due for publication 2019.

Flypast Magazine, Key Publishing. Various editions.

Fortress Singapore, The Battlefield Guide, Major Yap Siang Yong, Romen Bose, Angeline Pang. Ministry of Defence of Singapore. 1992.

Horsham, Town & Country, When the Siren Sounded, Cliff White, Cliff White Publications, 1995.

Mission Completed, ACM Sir Basil Embry, Methuen, 1957.

The Battle of Britain Then and Now. After the Battle, 1980.

The Bomber Command War Diaries, Martin Middlebrook and Chris Everitt, Viking 1985.

The Bristol Blenheim, A Complete History, Graham Warner, Crecy, 2002.

The Fighting Me109, Uwe Feist, Arms & Armour Press Ltd, 1988.

Royal Air Force Bomber Command Losses of the Second World War, 1939-1940, W R Chorley, 1992, Midland Counties Publications.

West Sussex County Times.

Wingless Victory, Anthony Richardson, Odhams Press. 1950.

Acknowledgements

Unfortunately since I started this project there are a number of people who deserve thanks but are no longer with us. There are also many that are still with us.

The first person to mention is Miss E M (May) Oakey – if she hadn't given me Harry's mess tunic I wouldn't have started. Next to thank is Elizabeth Bateman who saved the medals from being thrown away, and her husband Don; Cliff White for passing them on to me; Mr George Warman for giving me permission to access records and the loan of photographs; Miss May Jones and her mother for photographs and information; Mrs Julie Weston, George's daughter for getting in touch with the BBC – also for lunch and support on my visits; Mr Allen Flint for anecdotes; Mrs Lord (Miss Cook) ex Lower Beeding School Teacher for her pieces she sent me; Sandy Saunders 107 Squadron; Jack Coombes ex Collyer's School with Harry; The many other people of Lower Beeding who added small stories about Harry and a host of other minor players too numerous to mention by name; Mr Dan Mahoney for sending me copies of paperwork about his brother John; Mr Paish for talking about his uncle; the late Ed Stewart for his "Where are they now" slot on his afternoon programme.

I would also like to thank the Singapore National Cadet Corps for the chance to visit Singapore and for changing the training programme when I visited, to make it possible to do the wreath laying at Kranji. I also thank Sussex ACF for making the trip possible.

Peggy Ainsworth must also get a thank you for instilling the confidence and giving me a shove in the right direction to get on and finish this book.

With thanks also to Steve Lane for his help, encouragement and time spent on editing this book.

Thanks also to Momoko Matsuo-Grover of Rikkyo School for translation of Japanese text.

My wife Tracey played a large part in this in the early days, taking notes at National Archives and typing up the original draft and then the second one with changes along the way. Added to this all the letters she typed for me, and finally, my daughter Laura, for the title.

About the Author

David James Parker was born and brought up in Sussex. He has been interested in history, military in particular, from an early age. He became involved in this story some forty years ago when he was given a Royal Air Force jacket that belonged to Harry Warman. He had learnt a few facts about Harry from his father who had been at school when Harry was killed.

On starting secondary school (Forest Boys in Horsham) he was inspired by two very good history teachers, Mr Lloyd George Richardson, and Mr Chris Markes and Mr Bill Caudwell, a geography teacher who was also interested in the First World War. He went on his first battlefield tours with them in 1976 and again in 1977.

David started collecting items of militaria at ten years old when he found some medals in a bin. He has been giving talks about the First and Second World Wars for a number of years, using his extensive collections to illustrate these. He also gives talks on the Royal Observer Corps and his life as a chimney sweep.

David served in the Royal Observer Corps for twelve years before joining the Army Cadet Force as an instructor. He has had a few magazine articles published but this is his first venture into writing a book.

He is a local chimney sweep, well known in his area. This leads him to meet a vast number of interesting people who are pleased to share their stories with him. He also gets to see many historic cottages and larger houses.

The author
copyright Laura Parker